SCHOLASTIC



# SCHOLASTIC Go Grammar

## Course Book

### Level 7

The following pieces have been used with permission or are in public domain:
Page 75: Jon Stewart it's Commencement Address at the William and Mary College delivered on May 2004
Page 85: "My Watch: An Instructive Little Tale" by Mark Twain.
Page 100: "New Blue" by Paro Anand from *School Ahead.*
Page 102: *The Grasshopper's Run* by Siddhartha Sarma.
Page 105: "Haro Babu the Gentleman" by Shireshendu Mukhopodhyay, trans. Palash Baran Pal from *Funny and Funnier.*



Published by Scholastic India Pvt. Ltd.
A subsidiary of Scholastic Inc., New York, 10012 (USA)
*Publishers since 1920*, with international operations in Canada, Australia, New Zealand, the United Kingdom, India, and Hong Kong.



For information regarding permission, write to:
Scholastic India Pvt. Ltd.
A-27, Ground Floor, Bharti Sigma Centre
Infocity-1, Sector 34, Gurgaon (Haryana) 122001
Email: info_in@scholastic.asia

Series editor: Vivek Gopal
Illustrations: Rituparna Sarkar
Layout design and typesetting: Mansi Bansal

First edition: 2010
Reprinted: 2010, 2011 (thrice), 2012 (twice), 2013, 2014 (twice), 2015,
2016 (thrice), 2017 (twice), 2018, 2019 (thrice), 2021

ISBN-13: 978-81-8477-509-9

# Contents

# Introduction

Being aware of grammar rules enable us to communicate efficiently, clearly and understandably. As human beings, we can put sentences together even as children—we can all *do* grammar. But to be able to talk about how sentences are built, about the types of words and word groups that make up sentences—that is *knowing* about grammar. And *knowing* about grammar offers a window into the human mind and into our amazingly complex culture.

*Scholastic Go Grammar 6, 7* and *8* are a series of English grammar course books for the middle-school reader. These books have been created to provide a holistic approach to grammar and language usage that is geared towards practical application over rote memorisation. Simply put, *Scholastic Go Grammar* is a fun approach to grammar that is both instructive and edifying.

The *Scholastic Go Grammar* books

1. Include lesson plans that cover the written and spoken rules of grammar. These include practical solutions for problems that concern even native speakers of English.

2. Have extensive work sheets that engage the student with the rules and exceptions of the English language through practical instances

3. Encourage revision of topics covered in earlier books with more advanced exercises.

4. Include essays, poems, speeches from the finest writers around the world, with an added emphasis on Indian writers. The follow-up comprehension sections dissect how grammar allows these writers to express themselves as well as they do.

5. Incorporate activities that centre around community building in the classroom and events from the student's lives.

6. Provide an exhaustive compilation of supplemental material that is referential and provide a checklist of common writing errors.

7. Follow the current NCERT curriculum and pedagogical principles.

8. Enable educators to monitor students' progress over the course of a lesson through 'free writing' exercises and evaluation sheets provided.

An informative and motivating set of books, *Scholastic Go Grammar* will help students apply the rules of grammar in spoken and written English to make them effective and articulate communicators.

WORK SHEET 1

# Pronouns

Indefinite pronouns are words that replace nouns without specifying which noun they replace. An indefinite pronoun does not refer to any specific person, thing or amount. It can encompass a wide range of people, events or places.
For example: Can I have **another**?

## I Fill in the blanks with the correct personal pronouns.

1 ______________ is dreaming.

2 Candy is our new dog. ______________ is two years old.

3 Adam, Rajat and Maya are in town. ______________ live in Dubai.

4 What can ______________ tell me about yourself?

5 ______________ have offered to pay ______________ for the loss of her car.

## II Fill in the blanks with the correct reflexive pronouns.

1 He made the cabinet ______________.

2 We helped ______________ to the food.

3 The dog can defend ______________.

4 Aditya and Shantanu, if you want more pizza, help ______________.

5 She often talks to ______________.

6 Since I live alone, I often cook for ______________.

7 She blames ______________ for the accident.

8 Did you two clean up after ______________? No dinner until the room is spotless.

9 The children fought amongst ______________.

10 We have no choice but to do it ______________.

# Pronouns

We use reflexive pronouns when the subject and object of a sentence are the same person.

## I Fill in the blanks with **somebody**, **anybody**, **nobody**, **something**, **anything**, **nothing**, **somewhere**, **anywhere** or **nowhere**.

1 I know ____________ about Geeti that you may find interesting; but if I tell you, you must promise to keep it a secret.

2 ____________ ever wears a snazzy top hat anymore, and that's a real shame.

3 I spent the day ____________ near the beach.

4 Just goes to show you that you can't pigeonhole ____________.

5 ____________ scares him. He's very brave.

6 There is ____________ to sit here. Let's go ____________ else to eat.

7 I would love to be able to just go ____________.

8 May I have ____________ to eat, please?

9 They took him ____________ near London, but he managed to escape.

10 Please don't leave ____________ behind. We won't be coming back for a long time.

11 ____________ has to try to stop the panic.

12 If I wait for the financial situation to be perfect, I'll never go ____________.

13 There isn't ____________ you can do to help them. ____________ can help them.

14 I know that ____________ who hires me will understand if I am incompetent.

15 ____________ is ringing the bell. Find out who it is.

16 ____________ phoned while you were out, but he did not leave a name.

17 ____________ tells me that there is ____________ fishy going on.

18 I know that my interests and passions lie ____________ in education.

19 I would rather be ____________ than here.

20 "Is there ____________ at home?"

"I don't think there is ____________. The door is locked and the lights are off."

WORK SHEET 3

# Adjectives

Sometimes we use a noun to describe another noun. In that case, the first noun 'acts' just like an adjective. Possessive adjectives are adjectives that express possession or ownership of the action.

## I In each of the following sentences, indicate whether the word in bold is an adjective or a noun.

1 **Life** is not cheap. ☐ adjective ☐ noun

2 The viscount is a **close** friend of mine. ☐ adjective ☐ noun

3 The **Namibian** embassy is around the corner. ☐ adjective ☐ noun

4 Weekdays are **hectic** for me. ☐ adjective ☐ noun

5 My doctor is a man with little **patience**. ☐ adjective ☐ noun

## II Fill in the blanks with the correct possessive adjectives.

1 My friends brought ______________ child to my house for dinner.

2 Is this ______________ book?

3 The kids like ______________ presents.

4 He rides ______________ bicycle to school.

5 This is a lovely tree. ______________ leaves are a wonderful shade of orange.

WORK SHEET 4

# Adjectives

An adjective tells us more about a noun, and an adverb is a verb that describes.

## I Fill in the blanks with the correct words. Then indicate if each word is an adjective or an adverb.

1 He's a ______________ worker. He never stops. ☐ adjective ☐ adverb

2 He's lazy. He ______________ ever works. ☐ adjective ☐ adverb

3 It's 10 o'clock already. He's very ______________. Where can he be? ☐ adjective ☐ adverb

4 My train reached ______________. I'm sorry. ☐ adjective ☐ adverb

5 I haven't seen them ______________. ☐ adjective ☐ adverb

6 If I hear anything, I'll let you know ______________. ☐ adjective ☐ adverb

7 Mr Wiggum will be with you ______________. Please take a seat. ☐ adjective ☐ adverb

8 The ______________ man fell asleep. ☐ adjective ☐ adverb

9 You are too slow. You need to work ______________. ☐ adjective ☐ adverb

10 Please finish it ______________. We need it now. ☐ adjective ☐ adverb

11 This car takes turns too ______________. ☐ adjective ☐ adverb

12 He looked towards her and sighed ______________. ☐ adjective ☐ adverb

13 She gazed at her and gave a ______________ sigh. ☐ adjective ☐ adverb

14 After his meal, Guntes belched ______________. ☐ adjective ☐ adverb

15 Is the window open? I feel ______________. ☐ adjective ☐ adverb

WORK SHEET 5

# Adjectives

The comparative of a one-syllable adjective can be formed by adding **er** to the adjective.

## I Cross out the incorrect word(s) and write the correct word in the space provided.

1 Of all the players on the field, Raju is the faster. __________

2 This is the most beautifulest painting I have ever stolen. __________

3 They chose a dark shade of brown than their neighbours. __________

4 Of the two brothers, he is the most generous. __________

5 This is the most danger road in the area. __________

6 Sunday was the most enjoy day of the week. __________

7 This is the bestest cheesecake I've ever eaten. __________

8 I love you the mostest of all. __________

9 This will be the funnest part of the year. __________

10 This comedian was the most entertainingest. __________

11 This tree is the taller in the garden. __________

12 Shruti always has been gooder than her brother. __________

13 I did good on that practice test.

__________

14 We are going to need a biggest boat.

__________

WORK SHEET 6

# Adjectives

The superlative of a one-syllable adjective can be formed by adding an **est** to the adjective.

## I Use the correct form of the adjectives given to fill in the blanks.

| long | bad | clean | far | big | good |
|---|---|---|---|---|---|
| dangerous | cheap | expensive | luxurious | | |

1 Mercedes makes some of the most ______________ cars in the world.

2 That pie is terrible. In fact, it is the ______________ pie I've ever eaten.

3 Riding a motorbike is ______________ than driving a car.

4 The coffee in Italy is ______________ than the coffee you get anywhere else.

5 This room is fithy. The kitchen is much ______________.

6 My apartment is just as ______________ as yours.

7 If you buy the ______________, you won't get the best.

8 The aquarium in Venice is the ______________ in the world.

9 A week in Paris is ______________ than a week in Dharamshala.

10 The distance from school to my house is ______________ than the distance from yours.

11 This is the most______________ room in the hotel.

12 This class is boring. It feels like ______________ two hours of my life.

13 My friend Dave is ______________ lawyer in the country.

14 This is ______________ price we can find.

15 The Indian Railways is one of ______________ rail network in use.

WORK SHEET 7

# Articles

Remember that for **a** and **an**, the pronunciation of the succeeding word determines which article to use.

**I** **Fill in the blanks with the appropriate articles. Mark those sentences that do not require an article with an x.**

1 He spent five ______________ months on ______________ deserted island in 1982.

2 I will definitely go to ______________ college.

3 Do your ______________ friends go to ______________ arcade?

4 ______________ Sahara Desert is in ______________ Africa.

5 ______________ restaurant is on ______________ next street.

6 ______________ Mt. Kosciuszko is in ______________ Australia.

7 Go along ______________ this street and then take ______________ left and keep on ______________ right.

8 Can you speak ______________ Polish?

9 I'd like ______________ new pair of ______________ shoes for my trek.

10 Her ______________ brother is taking ______________ break.

11 Do you like ______________ animals?

12 I've won ______________ lottery!

13 Did ______________ you drink coconut water ______________ yesterday?

14 I should eat a lot of ______________ fruit and ______________ vegetables.

15 I can't wait for ______________ holidays to begin.

16 I saw ______________ eagle when I was travelling ______________.

17 ______________ Brad Pitt is ______________ most handsome man among my ______________ imaginary friends.

WORK SHEET 8

# Articles

**The** is used for specific things, offices, titles and famous landmarks.

## I Fill in the blanks with the appropriate articles. Mark those sentences that do not require an article with an x.

1 ____________ Ben's uncle is in ____________ hospital because he's very sick.

2 Go ____________ home and eat ____________ pizza.

3 I went to ____________ school by ____________ bike yesterday.

4 In my ____________ room you can find ____________ computer, ____________ bed, ____________ old wardrobe and ____________ desk. ____________ computer is new, ____________ bed is too small, ____________ wardrobe is too cluttered and ____________ desk belongs to my ____________ sister.

5 ____________ Canary Islands had better be filled with canaries.

6 My friend is married to ____________ actor.

7 You could end up choosing ____________ car that's not right for you.

8 If you're looking for ____________ place to eat, try there.

## II Insert the correct article.

1 I bought ____________ pair of trousers that were on sale.

2 She's planning ____________ trip to ____________ United Kingdom.

3 Where are all ____________ books?

4 What is it? Did you see ____________ elk?

5 I need ____________ honest appraisal before I can agree.

WORK SHEET 9

# Adverbs

The primary job or function of an adverb is to modify (give us more information about) verbs, adjectives and other adverbs.

## I Based on the percentage provided, rewrite the following with adverbs of frequency.

| | |
|---|---|
| 100% | always |
| | usually |
| 75% | frequently<br>often |
| 50% | sometimes |
| | occasionally |
| | rarely |
| 25% | seldom<br>hardly ever |
| 0% | never |

1 He (80%) listens to the radio.

______________________________

2 He (10%) gets angry.

______________________________

3 Where do you learn this stuff? I (0%) see you read.

______________________________

4 He's (70%) a friendly dog.

______________________________

5 I (100%) take a walk around this time.

______________________________

6 She'll (50%) take sugar in her coffee.

______________________________

7 They (90%) take the bus to school.

______________________________

8 It doesn't (80%) snow here in winter.

______________________________

9 Harry has (100%) wanted to own a restaurant.

______________________________

10 I (5%) read the fine print.

______________________________

11 I (0%) have the faintest idea what you say.

______________________________

12 We used to fight (75%) but now we just glare at each other across the hall.

______________________________

# Adverbs

Adverbs of manner are adjectives that take on the actions of verbs.

## I Fill in the blanks with the correct adverbs of manner.

1 The speaker looks upset. He's banging the table ______________ (angry).

2 We lost the match. Roy played ______________ (terrible).

3 Monica is a terrible driver. She drives ______________ (reckless).

4 Her friend is late. Carla has been waiting ______________ (impatient).

5 She read the e-mail ______________ (careful) before replying.

6 He's in trouble for answering the teacher ______________ (rude).

7 The puppy was ______________ (severe) injured by the fall.

8 The rhino plodded down the street ______________ (dreary).

9 He handed her her wig back and some roses ______________ (apologetic).

10 She ______________ (random) selected five students from the class.

## II Fill in the blanks with the appropriate adverbs of degree.

1 The food was ______________ spicy for me to eat.

2 I am just ______________ tired to keep working.

3 I can't afford that television. It's ______________ expensive.

4 The milk in this carton is green. It must be ______________ old.

5 There's ______________ any food left in the fridge.

# Prepositions

Prepositions are used before nouns to provide additional information.

## I Insert the correct prepositions in the following sentences.

1 ______________ his way to Mexico, he stopped over in Los Angeles.

2 Thanks ______________ all you've done for me.

3 You should spend your energy ______________ something worthwhile.

4 Is there anything ______________ sale at the mall this week? I don't have much money ______________ spend.

5 We're looking at some of the deals offered ______________ that ad.

6 Have you found a nice book ______________ her?

7 ______________ a rainy day, I like to stay at home.

8 In summer, hill stations are very popular with people who suffer ______________ the hot weather in their home towns.

9 John, do you remember Gaius? He's an old friend ______________ school.

10 Let's go ______________ a tour of the city.

11 Who is that man waving ______________?

12 Many animals are ______________ risk of extinction.

13 Switzerland is famous ______________ its watches.

14 You'd better change ______________ a lower gear when driving in bad weather.

15 Ours is the best car ______________ the market.

16 I went ______________ my father for a concert.

17 This story is similar ______________ the one she told us.

18 Find answers ______________ these questions if you can.

WORK SHEET 12

# Prepositions

Prepositions are used to show where something is located or when something happened. A sentence cannot end with a preposition.

## I Fill in the blanks with the correct prepositions.

1 This is an example ______________ alliteration.

2 The Kumars are not included ______________ this list.

3 He is searching ______________ a new job.

4 We're going on a trip ______________ two weeks.

5 It had been raining ______________ over two hours.

6 She didn't say anything ______________ the broken window.

7 What do you do ______________ the evenings?

8 He will be ready ______________ noon.

9 Would you like to go to the movie ______________ me?

10 The class starts ______________ 4 pm.

11 ______________ lunch, I'll start work on this project.

12 When I was young, I thought *Godzilla* ______________ *King Kong* was a fantastic film.

13 She's been ill ______________ this trip.

14 Her office is diagonally ______________ mine.

# Conjunctions

A conjunction joins words in a sentence. The three types of conjunctions are coordinating conjunctions, subordinating conjunctions and correlative conjunctions.

## I Complete the following sentences with the correct conjunctions.

1 Essays must be handed in by the deadline; __________ they will not be marked.

*a* obviously *b* otherwise *c* as a result

2 __________ she comes to school in her father's luxurious car, it does not seem the family is very wealthy.

*a* Nevertheless *b* Because *c* Even though

3 In order to try and reduce car use in the inner cities, the government has announced new restrictions on company parking spaces and __________, a new tax on individual car use.

*a* as well as *b* in addition *c* in the same way

4 Camels live in the desert, __________ dolphins live in the sea.

*a* however *b* jumping *c* whereas

5 I don't like strawberry ice cream. __________, I love chocolate flavour.

*a* whereas *b* however *c* even so

6 They grew up in Sudan; __________ their interest in Nubian art.

*a* hence *b* thus *c* also

7 You should always check the safety harness; __________ your parachute might not open.

*a* however *b* whereas *c* otherwise

8 I work every day. __________, I relax over the weekend.

*a* For example *b* However *c* Therefore

9 I don't think I'm qualified for the position. __________, I'm still going to apply.

*a* However *b* Therefore *c* As a result

10 He is really difficult to work with. __________, he will suddenly throw temper tantrums.

*a* Although *b* For example *c* However

WORK SHEET 14

# Conjunctions

A subordinating conjunction emphasises the idea in the main clause over the idea in the subordinate clause.

## I Connect the following sentences using the underlined words.

1 Shruti was very busy yesterday. She helped me move into a new apartment.

Despite the fact that: ______________________________.

Although: ______________________________.

However: ______________________________.

2 Vivek exercises vigorously. He can't lose weight.

Although: ______________________________.

Despite the fact that: ______________________________.

However: ______________________________.

3 Visitors are not allowed to park here. It is a private parking area.

Since: ______________________________.

Because: ______________________________.

Due to: ______________________________.

4 Hercules can't lift the box. He is very strong.

In spite of: ______________________________.

However: ______________________________.

But: ______________________________.

5 Tony Stark is rich. Clark Kent is poor.

Whereas: ______________________________.

In contrast to: ______________________________.

Unlike: ______________________________.

# Verbs

A verb is a word that shows action or state of being. The verb identifies what the subject is doing (or has done, or will do). Every sentence must have a verb.

- The fierce dog **bit** the burglar.
- She **is** a smart girl.

Verbs have two important functions:

- Some verbs put static subjects into motion.
- Other verbs provide additional information about the subject.

- My grumpy uncle snarled at the plate of cold food.

My grumpy uncle = static object; snarled = verb.

- The lizard splashed into Maya's soup.

The lizard = static object; splashed = verb.

Words can often have more than one function depending on the context in which they are used. Sometimes a word is a subject, sometimes a verb, sometimes a modifier.

One of the most important things about verbs is their relationship to time. Verbs indicate if something has already happened, if it will happen later, or if it is happening now.

Not only do verbs state the action taking place in a sentence, they also indicate its intensity.

- Some foods should not be eaten during a movie. Potato chips crunch too loudly, pickles smell and jalebis are messy to eat during a movie.
- The crunch of the potato chips drew angry glares from the rest of the audience.

**Crunch** is an action that we can do. We can **crunch** cockroaches under our shoes. Accountants can **crunch** numbers. In the first sentence, **crunch** is the action of the potato chip, so it is a verb.

Even though **crunch** is often a verb, it can also be a noun. The **crunch** of the potato chips, for example, is a thing, a sound that we can hear.

LESSON 1

# Verbs

## Imperative Verbs

The **imperative** form of the verb gives instructions or commands.

| be | Don't **be** lazy. |
|---|---|
| talk | **Talk** softly. |
| stand | **Stand** up straight! |

You can modulate the stress of an imperative verb and make it seem more akin to a request instead of a command by including words such as **do** or **please**.

- **Do** come to the party.
- **Please** sit down.

# Verbs

## Auxiliary Verbs

Auxiliary verbs give a more precise sense of time. They also give a sense of obligation or possibility.

### Time

We can indicate that an event is currently taking place.

- We **are eating** dinner.
- I **am listening** to you.

We can indicate that an event has already occured.

- They **have eaten** dinner.
- I **had listened** to you.

We can indicate that an event will take place at some point in the future.

- They **will eat** dinner.
- I **shall be listening** to your song.

### Obligation

Auxiliary verbs can also be used to indicate requests or obligations.

- You **must come** home after school.
- He **should be saving** his money.

### Possbility

Auxiliary verbs indicate events that might occur at some point in time.

- I **may go** out for lunch tomorrow.
- He **might meet** us later.

WORK SHEET 15

# Verbs

Imperative verbs may appear to have no obvious subject, but the subject is always implied.

## I Read each sentence. Cross out the incorrect verb and write the correct conjugation in the space provided.

1 My sister and her friend was down at the mall. ____________

2 A gaggle of geese have attacked me near the pond. ____________

3 The tiger as well as the keeper were missing from the zoo. ____________

4 Each of the camels have died in the desert. ____________

5 Nobody were able to finish the work before class. ____________

## II Pick the correct answer from the following.

1 Do you know Delhi at all?

No, this is the first time I ____________ here.

*a* was | *b* came

*c* am coming | *d* have been

2 Can I join your club?

You can when you ____________ a bit older.

*a* are | *b* will get

*c* are getting | *d* will have got

3 I'm sorry to keep you waiting.

Oh, not at all. I ____________ here only a few minutes.

*a* was | *b* had been

*c* have been | *d* will be

# Verbs

An auxiliary verb accompanies a main verb to indicate tense, possibility and obligation.

## I Pick the correct answer from the following.

1 I don't really work here; I ______________ until the new person arrives.

*a* just help out
*b* am just helping out
*c* have just helped out
*d* will just help out

2 If a book is ______________, it will surely ______________ the reader.

*a* interested; interest
*b* interesting; be interested
*c* interested; be interesting
*d* interesting; interest

3 He is late again today. I'll ______________ that he will not be late tomorrow.

*a* see it
*b* see to it
*c* will make it sure
*d* will make

4 The happy moment I had looked forward to ______________ at last.

*a* came
*b* coming
*c* come
*d* to come

5 Tom has just arrived, but I didn't know he ______________ until yesterday.

*a* had come
*b* came
*c* was coming
*d* will come

6 When I ______________ across a new word, I look it up in the dictionary.

*a* come
*b* am coming
*c* will come
*d* came

7 Everything ______________ by the time you get there.

*a* will have been ready
*b* had been ready
*c* was ready
*d* has been ready

# Verb Tenses

Verb tenses are used to indicate when an event begins or will terminate.

## Future Perfect

The future perfect refers to an action that will be completed in the future. We use this tense to project ourselves forward into the future and look back at an action that will be completed some time later than now.

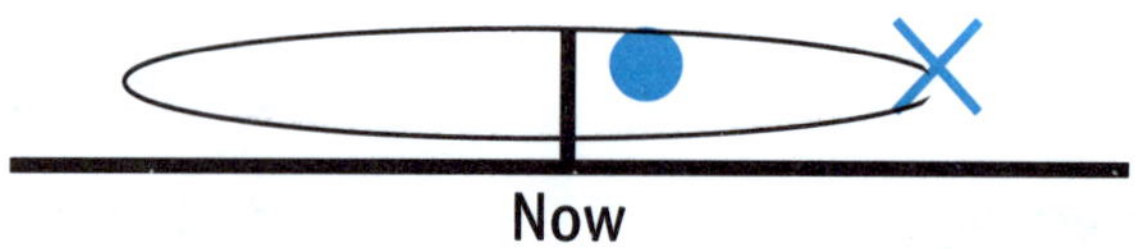


It is often used with an expression indicating time.

- By the time you read this, **I'll be halfway around the world.**
- **You will have submitted** your work by this time tomorrow.

The future perfect is composed of two elements: the simple future of the verb to have (will have) + the past participle of the main verb.

He will have eaten.

(subject) (verb form) (past participle)

| | Subject | Auxiliary verb | | Auxiliary verb | Main verb |
|---|---|---|---|---|---|
| Affirmative | I | will | | have | finished. |
| Negative | She | will | not | have | gone. |
| Interrogative | | Will | we | have | finished? |
| Interrogative negative | | Won't | he | have | eaten? |

# Verb Tenses

## Future Perfect Continuous

The future perfect continuous verb tense is used to

- state how long an action will have been in progress at a future time.
- state the results of an action or event in the future.
- represent a continuous action that started at some unknown point and continues into some point in the future.

A sentence in the future perfect continuous verb tense uses three auxiliary verbs and one main verb.

The future perfect continuous verb is formed by:

| subject | + | auxiliary verb | + | auxiliary verb | + | auxiliary verb | + | main verb |
|---|---|---|---|---|---|---|---|---|
| | | will | | have | | been | | verb + ing |

- You **will have been waiting** for more than two days when the results are finally announced.
- You **are going to have been waiting** for more than two hours when she finally arrives.

The future perfect continuous verb tense cannot be used with time clauses such as **when, while, by the time, soon, before, after, if, unless** and **until.**

- In May I will have been working here for five years.
- My mother will have been in teaching for thirty years next month.
- The children will have been playing for three hours in ten minutes.

## Future Perfect Continuous Forms

| Using **will** | | |
|---|---|---|
| **Positive** | **Negative** | **Question** |
| I will have been sleeping. | I will not have been sleeping. | Will I have been sleeping? |
| You will have been sleeping. | You will not have been sleeping. | Will you have been sleeping? |
| We will have been sleeping. | We will not have been sleeping. | Will we have been sleeping? |

# Verb Tenses

| Positive | Negative | Question |
|---|---|---|
| They will have been sleeping. | They will not have been sleeping. | Will they have been sleeping? |
| He will have been sleeping. | He will not have been sleeping. | Will he have been sleeping? |
| She will have been sleeping. | She will not have been sleeping. | Will she have been sleeping? |
| It will have been sleeping. | It will not have been sleeping. | Will it have been sleeping? |

| Using **be going to** | | |
|---|---|---|
| **Positive** | **Negative** | **Question** |
| I am going to have been sleeping. | I am not going to have been sleeping. | Am I going to have been sleeping? |
| You are going to have been sleeping. | You are not going to have been sleeping. | Are you going to have been sleeping? |
| We are going to have been sleeping. | We are not going to have been sleeping. | Are we going to have been sleeping? |
| They are going to have been sleeping. | They are not going to have been sleeping. | Are they going to have been sleeping? |
| He is going to have been sleeping. | He is not going to have been sleeping. | Is he going to have been sleeping? |
| She is going to have been sleeping. | She is not going to have been sleeping. | Is she going to have been sleeping? |
| It is going to have been sleeping. | It is not going to have been sleeping. | Is it going to have been sleeping? |

WORK SHEET 17

# Verb Tenses

The future perfect tense is used to show how long an action will have been in progress at a later time.

## I Fill in the blanks with either future perfect continuous or future perfect forms of the words in brackets.

1 **Simon:** Rachel is really going to speak Spanish well when she gets back from Mexico.

**Chuck:** Hopefully! She (take) ______________ classes for more than six months.

**Simon:** She is going to be able to speak Spanish with some of our Latin American clients.

**Chuck:** Good. Two clients from Peru (visit) ______________ us next month when Rachel returns. We need someone to pick them up from the airport.

2 **Vivek:** I am leaving!

**Nurse:** If you would please wait, the doctor will be with you shortly. The doctor is seeing another patient.

**Vivek:** The doctor has been seeing that patient for an hour. If I wait another ten minutes, I am sure he (still) ______________ be seeing her. By the time he's finally ready to see me, I (bleed) ______________ for more than two hours.

3 **Peter:** What are you going to be doing tomorrow?

**Debbie:** I (clean) ______________ my room.

**Peter:** Still? How long have you been cleaning your room?

**Debbie:** Forever. By the time I finish, I (rearrange) ______________ my room for over two weeks.

**Peter:** Too bad. I was going to ask if you wanted to see a movie. What about Sunday?

**Debbie:** Sorry, I (buy) ______________ furniture and (put) ______________ up curtains.

4 **Ben:** What are you going to be doing next year around this time?

**Mr Stein:** I (work) ______________ for a big law firm.

**Ben:** I didn't know you were leaving Delhi.

**Mr Stein:** I got an offer that I couldn't refuse. Besides, by the time I move, I (live) ______________ here for over twenty years. I think it's about time for a change.

WORK SHEET 18

# Verb Tenses

The future perfect tense has two forms: **will have done** and **going to have done**.

## I Complete the sentences using **will have** and past participle forms.

1 In the year 2100, life ______________ (become) more automated.

2 Computers ______________ (take over) many of the jobs that people do today.

3 The earth's supplies of oil, coal and gas ______________ (run out).

4 ______________ (scientists/find) other sources of energy?

5 How ______________ education ______________ (change)?

6 ______________ (we/find) a way to feed the entire population of the earth?

7 ______________ (you/master) archery by the time you return?

8 By now everyone ______________ (hear/news).

9 By Thursday, she ______________ (give up) all hope and then we can have the surprise party.

10 We ______________ (be) married for a year tomorrow.

11 Do you think you ______________ (finish) writing that book review by the time I return?

12 Don't call, she ______________ (left) for the airport by now.

WORK SHEET 19

# Verb Tenses

Many speakers often contract the subject and auxiliary verb when using the future perfect continuous tense.

## I Based on the information provided, complete the following sentences.

1 Dave and Bob are going to the cinema. The film begins at 5:30 and it is already 5:20. It will take them twenty minutes to get there.
When they get there, ____________________. (the film/already/start)

2 My dad always goes to bed at 11 o'clock. My uncle is going to visit him at 11:30 this evening.
When my uncle arrives, ____________________. (my dad/go/to bed)

3 Jordan is on holiday. He has very little money and he is spending too much too quickly.
Before the end of his holiday, ____________________. (he/spend/all his money)

4 Denis came to Microsoft nearly three years ago. Next Monday, it will be exactly three years since he started.
Next Monday ____________________. (he/be/here/exactly three years)

5 Next year is Parul and Varun's wedding anniversary. They ____________________ (marry) for twenty-five years.

6 Jane is from New Zealand. She is travelling around Europe at the moment. So far she has travelled about 1000 miles. By the end of the trip, ____________________ (she/travel) more than 3000 miles.

7 By next February I ____________________ (write) my third book.

8 I hope you ____________________ (not/forget) my name by tomorrow.

9 By next week we ____________________ (redecorate) the house.

10 Next July she ____________________ (be) dead for ten years.

11 I hope I ____________________ (not/make) a lot of mistakes in this exam when I finish it.

12 By the end of this year I ____________________ (drive) more than one hundred thousand kilometres in an autorickshaw.

WORK SHEET 20

# Verb Tenses

We use the future perfect continuous to talk about a lengthy action before some point in the future.

## I Use the correct form of the verbs in brackets to complete the following sentences.

1 I hope it ______________________ (stop) raining before the match starts.

2 I ______________________ (have) an operation when you come back.

3 By this time next week, I ______________________ (marry).

4 If nothing is done, one million species that are alive today ______________________ (become) extinct in twenty years.

5 The tropical rain forests ______________________ (disappear) in thirty years.

6 By the end of June, I ______________________ (live) in this hut for nine years.

7 I ______________________ (fly) to London for an hour at this time tomorrow.

8 At this time next week, I ______________________ (work) for this school for ten years.

9 When the bell rings, I ______________________ (teach) for eight hours today.

10 I ______________________ (wear) these glasses for five years next week.

11 I ______________________ (drive) this car for six years tomorrow.

12 At this time tomorrow, I ______________________ (take) a test for an hour.

13 At this time next year, I ______________________ (have) on holiday in Antalya for a week.

14 At this time next year, I ______________________ (live) in Istanbul for ten years.

15 By the time we get home, they ______________________ (play) football for half an hour.

16 She ______________________ (dance) for an hour by nine o'clock.

17 I ______________________ (learn) English for ten years by the end of this year.

18 Tomorrow is Aishwarya's birthday. She ______________________ (brood) in a corner.

WORK SHEET 21

# Verb Tenses

The future continuous tense indicates action at a specific moment in the future.

**I Complete the following sentences using the future continuous forms of the words in brackets.**

1 Next week, I (drive) ________________ to work.

2 This summer I (study) ________________ abroad.

3 Brian (sleep) ________________ on the sofa tonight.

4 It (rain) ________________ in Shillong at this time of the year.

5 I (go) ________________ to a movie with my parents in the evening.

6 My sister (visit) ________________ me during the winter vacation.

7 Harry (not/read) ________________ any comic books till his exams are over.

8 What (we/to do) ________________ at this time next year?

9 Left alone at home, the kids (cause) ________________ havoc.

10 Sara and Bunty (have) ________________ a great time travelling next summer.

11 Vivek (attend) ________________ the conference next month.

12 It's very late. She (sleep) ________________ when you call.

13 My mom (look) ________________ for bargains when she goes to the winter sale.

14 We (fly) ________________ over the Atlantic Ocean for three hours.

# Modal Verbs

Modals verbs are auxiliary verbs that express necessity or possibility. All the auxiliary verbs except **be**, **do** and **have** are called modals. Unlike other auxiliary verbs, modals only exist in their helping form; they cannot act alone as the main verb in a sentence.

## Common Modal Verbs

| can | could | may | might | must |
|---|---|---|---|---|
| ought to | shall | should | will | would |

There are some rules governing the use of modal verbs.

- Modal verbs do not take **s** in the third person.
  - He can speak French.
  - She should be here by now.
- We use **not** to make modal verbs negative, even in simple present and simple past tense.
  - He should not be running on the bus.
  - They might not come to class.
- Many modal verbs cannot be used in the past tense or the future tense.

# Modal Verbs

| Modal | Examples | Uses |
|---|---|---|
| can | They can't control their own pets. | ability/possibility |
| | We can't find it. | inability/impossibility |
| | Can I sit here? | asking for permission |
| | Can you help me? | request |
| could | Could I borrow your pen? | asking for permission |
| | Could you say it again more slowly? | request |
| | We could try to build it ourselves. | suggestion |
| | I think I could have another ice cream for lunch. | future possibility |
| | He gave up his old job so he could work for them. | ability in the past |
| may | May I have some more porridge please? | asking for permission |
| | China may become a major economic power. | future possibility |
| might | We'd better phone later they might be going out for dinner now. | present possibility |
| | They might give us a ten per cent discount. | future possibility |
| must | We must say goodbye now. | necessity/obligation |
| | They mustn't disturb the sleeping gorillas. | prohibition |
| ought to | We ought to employ a professional taxidermist. | saying what's right or correct |
| shall | Shall I help you with your luggage? | offer |
| | Shall we say 2.30 then? | suggestion |
| | Shall I buy that or will you? | asking what to do |
| should | We should sort out this problem at once. | saying what's right or correct |
| | I think we should check everything again. | recommending action |
| | The squid population should increase next year. | uncertain prediction |

# Modal Verbs

| Modal | Examples | Uses |
|---|---|---|
| will | I can't see any taxis so I'll walk. | instant decision |
| | I'll do that for you if you like. | offer |
| | I'll get back to you first thing on Monday. | promise |
| | The squid population will increase next year. | certain prediction |
| would | Would you mind if I brought a friend with me? | asking for permission |
| | Would you pass the salt please? | request |
| | Would you mind waiting a moment? | request |
| | "Would tomorrow suit you?" "That'd be fine." | making arrangements |
| | Would you like to play golf this Friday? | invitation |
| | "Would you prefer tea or coffee?" "I'd like tea please." | preferences |

# Modal Verbs

Modal verbs qualify statements, express need or suggest possible actions.

## I Write the correct modal verb for each of the sentences in the space provided.

1 Barney's flight from London took more than eleven hours. He ____________ be exhausted after such a long flight.

2 The book is optional. My professor said we could read it if we wanted to. But we ____________ read it if we don't want to.

3 I ____________ hear the singer because the crowd was cheering so loudly.

4 The phone isn't working. It ____________ damaged during the storm.

5 Ted: ____________ you hold your breath for more than a minute?
Phil: No, I can't.

6 You ____________ be rich to be a success. But it helps.

7 I've redone this maths problem at least twenty times, but my answer is wrong according to the book. The answer in the book ____________ be wrong!

8 You ____________ do the job if you didn't speak English fluently.

9 You ____________ worry so much. It doesn't do you any good. Either you pass the exam, or you don't.

10 You ____________ be joking! That can't be true.

11 You ____________ politely excuse yourself and leave the room once you have finished your work.

12 Jenny's engagement ring is enormous! It ____________ cost a fortune.

WORK SHEET 23

# Modal Verbs

Modal verbs modify other verbs to express intent.

## I Write the correct modal verb for each of the sentences in the space provided.

1 ____________ we move into the living room? It's cooler in there and there's a beautiful view of the lake.

2 If I had gone white-water rafting with my friends, I ____________ capsized in the river.

3 At first, my boss didn't want to hire Sam. But, because I had previously worked with Sam, I told my boss that he ____________ reconsider him for the position.

4 You ____________ take along some cash. The restaurant may not accept credit cards.

5 The robot ____________ turned on by flipping this switch.

6 I can't stand these people—I ____________ get out of here while you get rid of them.

7 You ____________ forget to pay the rent tomorrow. The landlord is very strict about paying on time.

8 Do you always have to say the first thing that pops into your head? ____________ you think before you speak?

9 Frank said he would come over right after tuitions; so they ____________ be here soon.

10 Yesterday, I ____________ study all day for my French final exam. I didn't get to sleep until after midnight.

11 We ____________ no longer suffer the terrible food here!

12 If I had gone to the university, I ____________ participated in their language induction programme.

13 The lamp ____________ be broken. Give it a rub to see if a genie pops out.

# Clauses

A clause is a group of words with a subject and verb.

There are two kinds of clauses:

## Principal clause

A principal or main clause consists of one complete idea. This is also known as an principal clause.

➩ I love grammar.

➩ He went home.

A simple sentence consists of one principal clause.

## Subordinate clause

A subordinate or dependent clause says more about the main idea in the principal clause. It depends on the principal clause to express its full meaning. It is linked to the principal clause by a conjunction or a relative pronoun. A subordinate clause is an incomplete sentence and makes no sense on its own.

➩ Because I love grammar

➩ Because I love grammar, I love this book.

➩ Since he went home

➩ Since he went home, he had time to finish his homework.

A complex sentence comprises a principal clause and one or more subordinate clauses.

Subordinate clauses are linked to the principal clause by conjunctions or relative pronouns, which is usually at the beginning of the clause.

Subordinate clauses can do the work of adverbs, nouns and adjectives.

- **Noun clauses:** Noun clauses do the work of nouns. They usually tell us what someone is doing, saying or feeling. Noun clauses can be placed anywhere in the sentence. A noun clause can replace any noun in a sentence and function as the subject or the object.

  ➩ He asked me *if I loved grammar*.

  ➩ She believed *that he had gone home*.

LESSON 4

# Clauses

⇒ *What his parents had got him for his birthday* the boy wondered.

We often use noun clauses in indirect speech.

⇒ Shruti said, "I want a holiday."

⇒ Shruti said *that she wanted a holiday*.

- **Adverbial clauses:** Adverbial clauses do the work of adverbs and tell us more about the verb. Like adverbs, adverbial clauses tell us how, where, why or for how long things happen. They are linked to the principal clause by conjunctions.

  ⇒ I'll do laundry *when I run out of clothes*.

  A subordinate clause is an adverb clause if you can replace it with an adverb.

  ⇒ I'll do laundry *later*.

  Adverbial clauses can be placed in the beginning, middle or end of a sentence.

- **Adjectival clauses:** Adjectival clauses do the work of adjectives and tell us more about people and things. They always follow the nouns that they describe. They are linked to the principal clause by the relative pronouns who, whom, which and that. They are also called relative clauses.

  Adverbial clauses can be restrictive or non-restrictive.

  - A **restrictive clause** begins with a relative pronoun, such as *that* or *who* or sometimes *which*. It specifies or restricts the noun.

    ⇒ The painting *that they painted in college* sold for a lot of money.

    This is the one painting that they painted in college and that is what sold for a lot of money.

  - A **non-restrictive clause** also begins with a relative pronoun, such as *which* or *who*, which adds extra information about the already-specified noun.

    ⇒ The painting, *which they painted in college*, sold for a lot of money.

    The painting, which sold for a lot of money, happened to be one that they had painted in

# Clauses

college. There may be other paintings that they had painted in college, but we are talking about a specific one that sold for a lot of money.

When using a restrictive clause, do not use a comma before the relative pronoun. When using a non-restrictive clause, always use a comma before the relative pronoun.

- The hungry children ate the bread that was not covered with mould.
- The hungry children ate the bread, which was not covered with mould.

In the first sentence, the restrictive clause means that the children ate only the bread that was not covered in mould but did not eat the bread that was covered in mould. In the second sentence, the non-restrictive clause indicates that the children ate all the bread. The bread was mould-free. It does suggest that there may be other food items that were covered in mould.

WORK SHEET 24

# Clauses

Every clause must have at least a subject and a verb.

**I For each sentence below, circle the noun clause and identify the type of noun clause as either direct object or indirect object.**

| | Sentence | | | | |
|---|---|---|---|---|---|
| 1 | That they would challenge the examination authorities in order to get better marks on an exam is on some students' minds. | ☐ | direct object | ☐ | indirect object |
| 2 | The director of the non-profit agency is anticipating that this year will reveal higher literacy rates and lower unemployment than in 2010. | ☐ | direct object | ☐ | indirect object |
| 3 | How much the economy will be affected was included in the results of a study conducted by a leading organisation. | ☐ | direct object | ☐ | indirect object |
| 4 | Whoever stole the diamond is still in the building. | ☐ | direct object | ☐ | indirect object |
| 5 | The company that tracks customer spending said their reports indicate sales have dropped to eight per cent this quarter compared to the last. | ☐ | direct object | ☐ | indirect object |
| 6 | Do you know what time it is? | ☐ | direct object | ☐ | indirect object |
| 7 | He thought that I had taken his car to school. | ☐ | direct object | ☐ | indirect object |
| 8 | That Denise hasn't starved is a miracle. | ☐ | direct object | ☐ | indirect object |
| 9 | What Payal said confounded me. | ☐ | direct object | ☐ | indirect object |
| 10 | We are all terrified that the final exam will be difficult. | ☐ | direct object | ☐ | indirect object |

WORK SHEET 25

# Clauses

An adjective clause acts as an adjective modifying a noun.

**I Underline the adjective clause in the following sentences and circle the word it modifies.**

1 I like a teacher who listens to his students.

2 The dog, who I loved dearly, was attacked by a bear last night.

3 Shantanu is a person who takes blame well.

4 All individuals with tickets will be admitted.

5 The shirt that you bought me fits like a tent.

6 The woman who baked the winning pie is my wife.

7 You called at a time when I was unable to answer.

8 These are not, in fact, the books that you are looking for.

9 Those who are willing to serve others will be rewarded.

10 One to whom much is given is expected to give much more in return.

11 My ship, which I loved like a woman, is destroyed.

12 The phone that I want to buy is finally on sale.

13 The house where my father grew up is now a sweet shop.

14 The song that I heard on the radio made me cry.

WORK SHEET 26

# Clauses

A adjectival clause provides additional information about something without starting another sentence.

## I Rewrite the following sentences as adjectival clauses.

1 I gave you a book. It was falling apart.

_______________

2 You live in a town. The town is very small.

_______________

3 The sweets are delicious. Shruti brought them yesterday.

_______________

4 The postcards haven't reached yet. I mailed them a week ago.

_______________

5 The football match was very dull. My friend played in it.

_______________

6 Avneet has a new dog. I don't trust it.

_______________

7 He lives in a house. The house is huge.

_______________

8 Sohinee wore a new shirt yesterday. Did you notice it?

_______________

9 A girl is talking to Martin. Do you know the girl?

_______________

10 Did you see the cat? It is lying on your bed.

_______________

11 There's a football match tomorrow. I think you shouldn't miss it.

_______________

# Punctuation

Punctuation is used to clarify and emphasise information as well as to tell us about the intonation and pauses to be observed when reading.

The four marks that we will be covering are:

**( ) Brackets**

Brackets enclose information that is relevant but separate from everything around it.

- The children (making a mess as usual) were fighting when she came home.
- The children were fighting when she came home.
  They were making a mess as usual.

**; Semicolon**

A punctuation mark indicating a pause typically between two main clauses that is more pronounced than that indicated by a comma. It is sometimes used in place of a full stop to separate sentences.

- This is a complete sentence; this is another one.

# Punctuation

## Dash

The dash is used in cases where there is a sudden break in the passage.

- He was a great man—in his own opinion.

The dash is also used to indicate a conclusion without expressing it.

- I'm sure he's a great man but—.

## Hyphen

The hyphen is a sign used to join words to indicate they have a combined meaning or that they are linked in the grammar of a sentence.

- This is an old-fashioned love song.

# Punctuation

Brackets enclose information. We sometimes use brackets to enclose numbers or letters used for listing items.

**I Remove the brackets from the following sentences to make one or more sentences.**

1 The sneakers (red and blue Air Jordans) were very expensive.

______________________________

2 The limousines (with tinted windows) could be carrying celebrities.

______________________________

3 The Sydney Opera House (at the entrance to the Sydney Harbour) is famous for its architectural design.

______________________________

4 Lady Gaga (who rarely shows emotion) was excited to meet the Queen.

______________________________

5 The shoes (made of expensive leather) get scuffed and dirty.

______________________________

6 The pancakes (blueberry and strawberry) were really delicious.

______________________________

7 The packages (wrapped in brown paper) could be a bomb.

______________________________

8 Aishwarya (brooding in a corner) is celebrating her birthday.

______________________________

WORK SHEET 28

# Punctuation

Full stops go inside the brackets only if an entire sentence is inside the brackets.

## I The following sentences have brackets that are missing. Rewrite them correctly.

1 The picture on the previous page is of a tractor.

______________________________

2 Members of the constabulary in England sometimes called "peelers" get their nickname from Sir Robert Peel.

______________________________

3 The Taj Mahal located in Agra is not made entirely out of marble.

______________________________

4 The Delhi Daredevils based in Delhi is a famous cricket team.

______________________________

5 The teacher who was new could not control the class.

______________________________

6 A report on education April 2005 shows that the level of literacy is only rising in urban areas.

______________________________

7 I visited Goa which was full of tourists on my way south.

______________________________

8 You can eat almost anything when travelling if you observe simple rules for instance avoiding unbottled or unboiled water.

______________________________

WORK SHEET 29

# Punctuation

A few grammarians feel that brackets can be replaced by commas in almost all cases.

**I Punctuate the following sentences. Keep in mind that often there is more than one way to punctuate a sentence correctly.**

1 When a pet dies part of yourself dies too

2 We took photographs of the patron saint of lost causes Saint Jude

3 Picture this a man deep in the forest gorges on the food around him fruits berries anything sweet and edible

4 Last week we read *The Adventures of Onion Choppers* a book by Aishwarya Subramanian

5 Our three friends Larry Curly and Moe have decided to enter show business

6 When in doubt mumble when in trouble panic

7 Childrens love for McDonalds rests in part on the sense of familiarity associated with all McDonalds restaurant settings across the world

8 Some batsmen hit the ball and stand waiting for it to land others run to try and score runs

9 Hurling which has been the national sport of Ireland since legendary times is to Indian eyes like a football game played at hockey speed

10 The train its metal wheels squealing as they spin along the rusted tracks rolls more slowly now

WORK SHEET 30

# Punctuation

A semicolon is sometimes used in place of a full stop to separate two sentences usually where the conjunction has been left out.

## I Rewrite the following using a semicolon to replace the conjunction.

1 It was raining so I had to take an umbrella.

______________________________

2 I felt like a fool because I got on the wrong bus.

______________________________

3 My children run amuck in the living room because they are energetic.

______________________________

4 Bartleby liked the first film the best because he thought the second one was rubbish.

______________________________

5 I liked *Ulysses* as it was a pleasure to read.

______________________________

# Transitional Words and Phrases

Transitional words and phrases show the association between thoughts, sentences or paragraphs and they help make writing smoother.

Read the following paragraph:

The first meeting was a disaster. It was a complete debacle. I was intrigued by what my friend Sonia had told me about Mr Roy; she had said that he was charming and open to meeting someone new. He had recently seen me at a conference and had wanted to meet me. Sonia said that he was an avid reader; we would have lots to talk about. He liked swimming; that was a plus for me. I asked to meet Mr Roy.

There is nothing wrong with the grammar, punctuation or spelling in the above paragraph, but it is choppy and boring. Read the same paragraph after transitional words and phrases (underlined) have been added.

The meeting was more than a disaster. In fact, it was clearly a complete debacle. At first, I was somewhat intrigued by what my friend Sonia had told me about Mr Roy; namely, she had said he was quite charming and also open to meeting someone new. In fact, he had recently seen me in the distance at a conference and had wanted to meet me. Sonia said that he was quite an avid reader for one thing; therefore, we would have lots to talk about. In addition, he liked swimming; that was certainly a plus for me. I eventually agreed to meet Mr Roy on Saturday.

By including transitional words and phrases, the movement from one idea to another is much smoother and the language of the paragraph has some life in it.

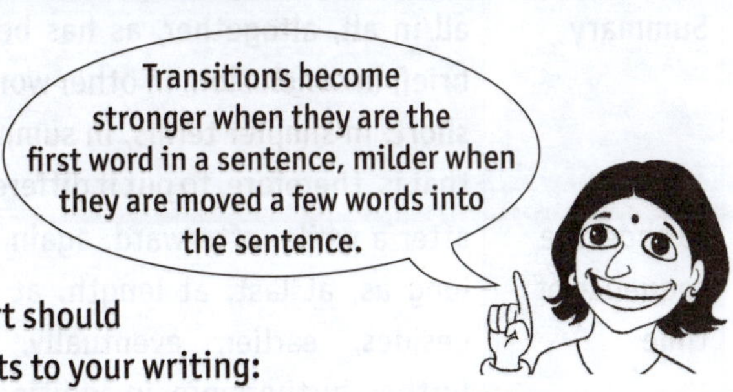


Transitional words and phrases can be divided into categories according to their use. The following chart should give you lots of ideas for adding transitional elements to your writing:

| Function | Transitional words | Examples |
|---|---|---|
| Addition | again, also, and, and then, besides, equally important, finally, first, further, furthermore, in addition, in the first place, last, moreover, next, second, still, too | It was great to meet old friends **again**. |

# Transitional Words and Phrases

| Function | Transitional words | Examples |
|---|---|---|
| Comparison | also, in the same way, likewise, similarly | Most of the clowns in the circus were **similarly** dressed. |
| Concession | granted, naturally, of course | **Granted**, life can be hard, but consider the alternative. |
| Contrast | although, and yet, at the same time, but at the same time, despite that, even so, even though, for all that, however, in contrast, in spite of, instead, nevertheless, notwithstanding, on the contrary, on the other hand, otherwise, regardless, still, though, yet | Dennis knew the cabbage was rotten, but he ate it **regardless.** |
| Emphasis | certainly, indeed, in fact, of course | "Did you rob the little, old lady?" "**Indeed**, I did." |
| For example | after all, as an illustration, even, for example, for instance, indeed, in fact, in other words, in short, it is true, of course, namely, specifically, that is, to illustrate, thus, truly | The simple sentence served Hemingway well; **after all**, he did get a Nobel Prize in Literature. |
| Summary | all in all, altogether, as has been said, finally, in brief, in conclusion, in other words, in particular, in short, in simpler terms, in summary, on the whole, that is, therefore, to put it differently, to summarise | The infinitive is a single unit and, **therefore**, should not be split. |
| To show the sequence of time | after a while, afterward, again, also, and then, as long as, at last, at length, at that time, before, besides, earlier, eventually, finally, formerly, further, furthermore, in addition, in the first place, in the past, last, lately, meanwhile, moreover, next, now, presently, second, shortly, simultaneously, since, so far, soon, still, subsequently, then, thereafter, too, until, until now, when | She **eventually** rose to the position of vice-president. |

Note that some words appear with more than one function.

WORK SHEET 31

# Transitional Words and Phrases

Transitional words and phrases can join two simple sentences to form a compound sentence.

## I Join these two sentences into one using transitional words or phrases.

1 The Gopals were having a party.
Their daughter was getting engaged.

______________________________________________

2 The police issued a warning on the radio.
A dangerous prisoner had escaped from prison.

______________________________________________

3 The car broke down.
Justin went to find help.

______________________________________________

4 Mansi heard a strange sound.
She became very frightened.

______________________________________________

5 The policeman told her not to look back.
She could not help it.

______________________________________________

6 I didn't want to hurt his feelings.
His tattoo looks more like a pony than a fierce dragon.

______________________________________________

7 I'm stuck outside in the rain getting wet.
I want an umbrella.

______________________________________________

8 Opening the box, Nandita was horrified to see thousands of spiders pour out.
She ran screaming into the street.

______________________________________________

WORK SHEET 32

# Transitional Words and Phrases

Transitional words are used to imply sequence and importance.

**I Fill in the blanks with the appropriate transitional word or phrase. Refer to the supplemental page for possible words.**

1 Amitava agreed to work on Saturday ______________ he could take Monday off.

2 Tom loaned Huck his pipe ______________ to gain his trust.

3 ______________ most cars are quite loud, the Prius, which is electric, is rather quiet.

4 I've been to several Japanese cities ______________ Osaka, Kobe and Sapporo.

5 ______________ his above-average weight, Justin could not skydive safely.

6 ______________ the issue of a tax-free zone, I believe people might shop more.

7 My father was a small man. ______________, I'm shorter than average.

8 I'm an egoist. ______________ I believe people are naturally selfish.

9 ______________ to page 3 of this essay, many poor people lack proper medical care.

10 They went to Rome. After that they went to Paris. ______________ they went to Prague.

11 Poets talk a lot. ______________, my friend Bhuvan.

12 Chris is always late for class. ______________, the teacher scolds him.

13 That country is having a civil war. ______________, many people have died.

14 I locked the door ______________ someone steals my stereo.

# Sentences

A sentence is a group of words that conveys meaning when put together.

## Simple Sentences

A simple sentence is also an principal clause. It contains a subject and a verb and it expresses a complete thought. In the following simple sentences, subjects are in **bold** and verbs are in *italics*:

- **Everyone** *loves* grammar.
- **Vivek** *wants* a pie.
- **Vandana** *should* bake a pie for Vivek.

## Compound Sentences

A compound sentence contains two principal clauses joined by coordinators like **for**, **and**, **nor**, **but**, **or**, **yet** and **so.** In the following sentences, subjects are in **bold**, verbs are in *italics* and coordinators are ***bold*** and ***italics.***

- **I** *opened* the fridge ***and*** *found* nothing there.
- **They** *walked* to the beach ***and*** *had* a swim.

The above are compound sentences. Each sentence contains two principal clauses and is joined by a coordinator with a comma preceding it. Note how the coordinators can change the relationship between the clauses.

## Complex Sentences

A complex sentence has an principal clause joined by one or more subordinate clauses. A complex sentence always has a subordinator such as **because**, **since**, **after**, **although** or **when** or a relative pronoun such as **that**, **who** or **which.**

- The **man** *returned* the book after he *noticed* an error.
- After **they** *finished* studying, **Rohan** and **Maria** *went* to see a movie.

Complex sentences can sometimes combine multiple sentences into one without a subordinator, but with a comma.

# Sentences

➩ Falstaff cried. He felt terrible for what he had done. He fell on his knees.

➩ Falstaff, feeling terrible for what he had done, fell on his knees and cried.

## Complex-compound sentences

Complex-compound sentences are made up of two principal clauses with one or more subordinate clauses.

➩ The dog lived in the garden, but the puppy, who barked more, lived inside the house.

Principal clauses:

- The dog lived in the garden.
- The puppy lived inside the house.

Subordinate clause:

- *who barked more*

➩ Lopa visited the fair and bought the doll that was on display.

(principal clause) (principal clause) (subordinate clause)

# Sentences

- John went to school, while James remained at home because he had a sore throat.
  - John went to school, (principal clause)
  - while James remained at home (principal clause)
  - because he had a sore throat. (subordinate clause)

- When they reached the bank where the jewels were kept, the gang of robbers stole a car and began planning the robbery.
  - When they reached the bank (subordinate clause)
  - where the jewels were kept, (subordinate clause)
  - the gang of robbers stole a car (principal clause)
  - and began planning the robbery. (principal clause)

- Mansi will complete the task and move on the next one, when she is advised that it is time to do so.
  - Mansi will complete the task (principal clause)
  - and move on the next one, (principal clause)
  - when she is advised (subordinate clause)
  - that it is time to do so. (subordinate clause)

WORK SHEET 33

# Sentences

Complex and complex-compound sentences must always have a subordinator or a relative pronoun.

## I Identify the structure of these sentences as simple (S), compound (C), complex (CX) or compound-complex (CCX).

1 Great literature stirs the imagination; furthermore, it challenges the reader's intelligence.

2 Great literature that stirs the senses will remain popular for many generations of readers.

3 When my son ran out of money for petrol, I told him to get his bicycle out of the garage.

4 Panamik has the filthiest water of all the lakes in the country.

5 Twelve tasks faced Hercules when he returned; he slew the Nemean Lion first.

6 We had read the assignment, but we did not understand it because the instructions were unclear.

7 The electricity bill that I received was shockingly high.

8 The ancient heater in our house stopped working sometime during the coldest night of the year.

9 On a stage of this size, you must speak louder, or your audience will not hear you.

10 The students at our school were dismissed early, but nobody in my class went home early.

11 The latest report from the hospital showed a slight improvement in her condition.

12 My neighbour's stories are always very long and boring, but we're forced to listen out of politeness.

13 The new car he bought last month is already at the mechanic's.

14 Can you explain to me why our four-toed shoes were a financial failure?

15 Luis was enthusiastic about his new job.

WORK SHEET 34

# Sentences

Complex-compound sentences are made up of two principal clauses with one or more subordinate clauses.

## I Rewrite the following sentences as complex-compound sentences.

1 Rachel gave me a cake recipe. I did not use it. Her cake tasted funny.

2 He went to the market. He needed more milk. Then he made pudding.

3 I will not drink the coffee. It is too cold. Please brew a fresh pot.

4 I prefer watching action movies. I recently watched a thriller. I enjoyed it very much.

5 I forgot her birthday. I suddenly remembered. I sent a card.

6 The team captain scored the final goal. The fans cheered. They won the championship.

7 Mansi works. I eat potato chips. And write.

8 Sheetal eats breakfast. Then she goes to school or goes for music class.

9 James said enough. We all agreed.

10 Dad went golfing. Mom stayed home. She wanted to be there in case the cat returned.

# Dangling Modifiers

A modifier is a word, especially an adjective or noun that restricts or adds to the sense of the main noun.

➩ **Good** and **family** in a good family home.

Incorrect placement or arrangement of words can turn the most well-crafted statement into a puddle of inanity.

➩ There is a large fountain at the end of the garden carved out of marble.

Unless you have the world's worst taste in outdoor design, that sentence should read:

➩ There is a large fountain carved out of marble at the end of the garden.

When you read the following sentences, ask yourself, "Who is doing what to whom?" This will help make the original meaning clear.

➩ I gave a table to my mother made of elephant legs.

The problem here is that the subject of the verb is not made clear. This is called a dangling modifier because it's left 'dangling' without a clear antecedent.

➩ Flitting gaily from flower to flower, the wrestler watched the bee.

In the example above, "flitting" is clearly intended to go with "bee"—bees, after all, naturally flit—but because the closest noun to "flitting" is "the wrestler," the sentence seems to suggest that the athlete is doing the flitting, not the bee. The sentence should read, "The wrestler watched the bee flitting gaily from flower to flower."

Fixing dangling modifiers:

1. Understand what dangling modifiers and misplaced modifiers are. A dangling modifier just dangles at the beginning of the sentence, unconnected to any logical subject. A misplaced modifier is just that—misplaced. All the elements of speech are there, but are not properly linked.

# Dangling Modifiers

2. Watch out for **-ing** words near the beginning of a sentence. These often signal a dangling modifier. Take a look at this sentence:

   ➩ When writing, modifiers can help you clarify your points.

   The first part of the sentence, "When writing" is a dangling modifier. The word that follows it—"modifiers" doesn't make any sense. Modifiers don't write. You do. What it should read is

   ➩ When you are writing, modifiers can help you clarify your points.

3. We can fix dangling modifiers by adding a subject to the modifier itself, or by adding a logical subject immediately after the modifier. The above example could also be written as:

   ➩ When writing, you can use modifiers to help you clarify your points.

4. Be careful when using passive verbs. Passive verbs often move the subject further along the sentence. If your passive sentence is dangling, consider making it active.

5. Watch out for words like **only**, **almost**, **even** and **nearly**, because these are the most commonly misplaced modifiers. Ensure they are placed before the subject being described. For instance,

   ➩ Clarabelle only ate two cookies.

   The modifier, "only," appears before "ate," which suggests that the writer expected Clarabelle to devour, or demolish two cookies—not just eat them. Logic would dictate that the writer intended to clarify the number of cookies Clarabelle ate. We can fix this by moving the modifier before the noun it should modify:

   ➩ Clarabelle ate only two cookies.

WORK SHEET 35

# Dangling Modifiers

A dangling modifier is a phrase or clause that says something different from what is meant because words are left out. The meaning of the sentence, therefore, is left dangling.

## I Rewrite each of the following to correct the dangling modifier.

1 Blown away by the tornado, the family could not find the roof of their house.

_______________

2 Painting by the street light, the picture was completed in record time.

_______________

3 Talking on his cell phone and driving at the same time, the policeman fined Kunal.

_______________

4 Made of crystal, I handled the glasses with care.

_______________

5 Driving through the sanctuary, several bears were seen.

_______________

6 Riding my bike home, an angry dog chased me.

_______________

7 Having eaten my meal, the waiter gave me the bill.

_______________

8 At the age of eight, my grandfather died.

_______________

9 Rushing to catch the bus, Chuck's wallet fell out of his pocket.

_______________

10 Cleaning his room, many cobwebs were found by Ashish.

_______________

WORK SHEET 36

# Dangling Modifiers

When a modifier 'dangles' so that the sentence is meaningless or means something other than your intent, restate it and add the words it needs in order to make sense.

## I Rewrite the following sentences in the correct order.

1 The policeman found a child crying for his mother who was forty years old.

_______________

2 The princess arrived on a ship dressed in a pink dress.

_______________

3 The car was finally sold by my father which is old and rusty.

_______________

4 The caveman was found a short distance from a half-eaten *Tyrannosaurus rex*.

_______________

5 The mechanic tried to inflate the car tyre with the lazy eye.

_______________

6 He assassinated the president with the scimitar.

_______________

7 The post-it note was read by the robot that was stuck to the board.

_______________

8 The florist sold the bouquet with one leg.

_______________

9 The aliens probed the captured humans who were green and slimy.

_______________

10 The robber ran from the policeman, still holding the money in his hands.

_______________

# Proverbs

Proverbs are short expressions or sayings that have become popularly known over time. Proverbs are considered to contain basic truths relating to human experiences.

- Good things come to those who wait.

Proverbs have been called the shortest art form. They provide vivid imagery to impart life lessons. The origin is usually unclear.

The proverb, "Don't buy a pig in a poke," could have originated as sound advice in medieval Europe, where dishonest merchants substituted cats for pigs. A poke was the bag for carrying goods and naive shoppers, who thought they were buying a pig in a poke, might discover they'd bought a cat instead. Now, the expression is used to warn someone not to accept or buy anything without examining it.

Since proverbs don't refer to a specific context, they are almost always in the simple present or present continuous tense.

- A ship in the harbour is safe, but that is not what ships are built for.

Proverbs are often metaphorical in nature, an aspect that makes them very pliable for use in writing. The above proverb while seeming like practical nautical advice is also a metaphor on risk taking.

- We still might finish in time for the deadline, but **there's many a slip twixt the cup and the lip.**

If you are unfamiliar with a proverb, use the context in which it is used to help you guess the meaning. The **but** warns us that the succeeding line is in contrast to what has been said before, so we can infer that the expression "many a slip twixt the cup and the lip" is a warning or caution regarding overconfidence.

While proverbs might be considered truisms, they are still based on old, loosely held cultural beliefs. As a result, you will find just as many proverbs that contradict each other.

- Don't judge a book by its cover.
- Clothes make the man.

Of course, not everything is written in stone. After all when was the last time you had to purchase a pig? Or wield a sword? A fun exercise might be to try and update some older proverbs, like:

- **Don't store all your data on one disk** instead of **Don't put all your eggs in one basket.**

WORK SHEET 37

# Proverbs

A proverb is a short, well-known pithy saying, stating a general truth or piece of advice.

## I Rewrite the following proverbs by using common examples.

1 Beware of Greeks bearing gifts.

2 If you want to see the valley, you'll have to climb the hills.

3 Rome wasn't built in a day.

4 A penny saved is a penny earned.

5 You can't make a silk purse out of a sow's ear.

6 Make hay while the sun shines.

7 Don't count your eggs before they hatch.

8 Too many cooks spoil the broth.

# Proverbs

Proverbs seldom have specific subjects as they are metaphoric in nature.

## I Match the proverbs given to their meanings.

| Proverbs | | Meanings | |
|---|---|---|---|
| 1 | A leopard can't change its spots. | *a* | If you can't see someone or something, you soon forget about them. |
| 2 | Kill two birds with one stone. | *b* | Achieve two goals with one action. |
| 3 | Too many cooks spoil the broth. | *c* | If you want to know about someone look at his friends. |
| 4 | Out of sight, out of mind. | *d* | Some people never change. |
| 5 | A double-edged sword. | *e* | A showy article may not be valuable. |
| 6 | A person is known by the company he keeps. | *f* | Sometimes it is better for one person to do something, rather than lots of people. |
| 7 | Birds of a feather, flock together. | *g* | Something that can be both an advantage and a disadvantage. |
| 8 | A wolf in sheep's clothing. | *h* | Something dangerous, but looks innocent. |
| 9 | All that glitters is not gold. | *i* | Two people can get on better when there's no one else. |
| 10 | Two's company, three's a crowd. | *j* | People tend to join people with similar interests/outlooks. |

# Proverbs

Because proverbs change over time, the wording may vary slightly but the meanings remain consistent.

**I Match the proverb with the proverb whose meaning appears contradictory.**

| | | | |
|---|---|---|---|
| 1 | Look before you leap. | *a* | Fools seldom differ. |
| 2 | If at first you don't succeed, try, try again. | *b* | Nothing ventured, nothing gained. |
| 3 | Absence makes the heart grow fonder. | *c* | He who hesitates is lost. |
| 4 | Never put off till tomorrow what you can do today. | *d* | Out of sight, out of mind. |
| 5 | Great minds think alike. | *e* | Opposites attract. |
| 6 | Haste makes waste. | *f* | Beware of Greeks bearing gifts. |
| 7 | You're never too old to learn. | *g* | Paddle your own canoe. |
| 8 | Birds of a feather flock together. | *h* | The sqweaky wheel gets the grease. |
| 9 | It's better to be safe than sorry. | *i* | Don't cross the bridge until you come to it. |
| 10 | Don't look a gift horse in the mouth. | *j* | You can't teach an old dog new tricks. |
| 11 | Silence is golden. | *k* | Time waits for no man. |
| 12 | Hitch your wagon to a star. | *l* | Don't beat your head against a stone wall. |

# Revision 1

**I** **Try to solve the questions given. If you are unsure of your answer, check the hint provided.**

**1** Which of the following two phrases is correct?

*a* Pooja and Arvind's car ☐

*b* Pooja's and Arvind's car ☐

But if the entity had been cars, the correct wording would be *Pooja's* and *Arvind's* cars. Each person has a car—and each gets his or her own. If two people share ownership of a single entity—in this case, the car—then only the second noun shows the possessive ending. In the example above, Pooja may be the fortunate co-owner of a car, but she does not get her own.

**2** If you have one sister, which of the following sentences is correctly punctuated?

*a* My sister Jean has been working on a play at her local library. ______

*b* My sister, Jean, has been working on a play at her local library. ______

The use of commas tells us that the writer has just one sister, and her name is Jean. In the first answer, the absence of commas tells us that the writer has more than one sister.

**3** Neither of the boys ______________ going to be there tonight.

*a* is ☐

*b* are ☐

The pronoun *neither* is the subject of the sentence and is singular; therefore, it requires a singular verb.

**4** Which of the sentences below is correct?

*a* The first puppy in the kennel to be sold was their's; our's took two months longer. ☐

*b* The first puppy in the kennel to be sold was theirs; our's took two months longer. ☐

*c* The first puppy in the kennel to be sold was theirs; ours took two months longer. ☐

Keep in mind which puppy is being talked about.

# Revision 1

5 ______________ either of you available to give the talk tomorrow?

*a* Are *b* Is

The pronoun *either* is the subject and is singular, so it requires a singular verb.

6 Which of the following sentences is correct?

*a* The children's favourite story was yours. ☐

*b* The children's favourite story was your's. ☐

Possessive pronouns never contain apostrophes.

7 She spoke to Swati and ______________ about the upcoming trip.

*a* me *b* I *c* myself

The subject is not Swati and you, but you. How would you answer "She spoke to ________ about the upcoming trip"?

8 Which of the following sentences is correct?

*a* This book is not only boring but also costs a lot. ☐

*b* This book is not only boring but also expensive. ☐

Whenever you use *not only... but also*, the grammatical elements linked by the expression must be the same. *Boring* is an adjective. Therefore, what follows *but also* should also be an adjective.

9 Which of the following sentences is correct?

*a* Overcome with homesickness, the student's work suffered. ☐

*b* Overcome with homesickness, the student found it hard to concentrate on his work. ☐

*c* Overcome with homesickness, work was difficult for the student. ☐

Pay close attention to the noun that is being modified.

# Revision 1

## II Fill in the blanks with the correct verb tense.

1 This time tomorrow, Jay ______________ on a beach in Goa. (vacation)

2 Wake me up by eight o'clock. I ______________ long enough by then. (sleep)

3 Sure, I can give you a lift. I ______________ that way anyway. (drive)

4 It's amazing that when we get to Sydney, ______________ half way round the world. (fly)

5 Don't call me between 6 and 8. I ______________ a nap then. (have)

6 Pick me up after 8 o'clock. We ______________ breakfast by then. (finish)

7 Tomorrow afternoon we're going to play cricket from 2 o'clock until 4.30. So at 4 o'clock, we ______________ cricket. (play)

8 Do you think you ______________ the same job ten years from now? (still/do)

9 By the time you return, I ______________ the house from top to bottom. (clean)

10 If I ______________ taller, I'd be better at basketball. (be)

## III Complete the following sentences with one of the following words.

can could may might should ought to shall will

1 The interview stated that he ______________ play the piano at the age of three.

2 You ______________ take an umbrella in case it starts to pour.

3 It's going to rain all afternoon. ______________ we see a movie instead?

4 Scott ______________ be 24 at the end of this month.

5 Chitra said traffic is heavy, and so she ______________ be late for the meeting.

6 You look lost. ______________ I help you?

7 You didn't pay for the ticket? You ______________ be ashamed of yourself!

8 I don't know the answer to this question. ____________ I look at your solution?

9 You ____________ enter the judge's chamber.

10 There ____________ be a law against that.

## IV Fill in the blanks with the correct conjunction.

1 I need a desk to myself ____________ I can get some work done.

2 Make a note of it ____________ you don't forget.

3 ____________ he was the most qualified, he didn't get the position.

4 ____________ you already know Margaret, you should go to meet her at the station.

5 I don't know ____________ I'll be back.

6 I haven't heard from him ____________ last month.

7 She continued to study ____________ she was exhausted.

8 I'm not leaving ____________ I get an apology from you.

9 I don't mind if you go out ____________ you're back in time for lunch.

10 ____________ I don't agree with what you say, I will defend your right to say it.

## V Rewrite the following sentences in the passive voice.

1 Fred asked Barney for a loan.

____________

2 The company forbids smoking.

____________

3 The police arrested six people.

____________

4 Frank Sinatra sang "My Way".

______________________________

5 He might come see you tomorrow.

______________________________

6 They erected that statue in 1954.

______________________________

7 Did the story interest you?

______________________________

8 I prepared the refreshments.

______________________________

9 The students will finish the course by August.

______________________________

10 They make these toys out of wood.

______________________________

LESSON 10

# Direct and Indirect Speech

## Direct Speech

Repeating **exactly** what someone has said or written is called direct speech (sometimes called quoted speech). We place the statement within quotation marks and do not alter what was said or written.

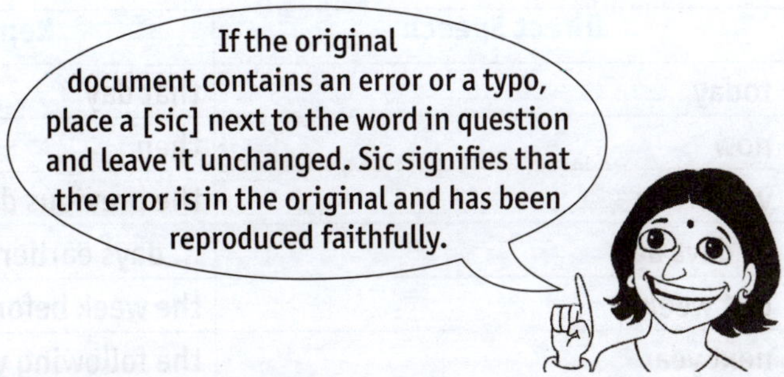


## Indirect Speech

Indirect speech (sometimes called reported speech) reports or recreates what has been said. It is understood to be the speaker's version of the events and neither requires quotation marks to enclose what the person said nor does it have to be word for word.

When reporting speech, the tense usually changes. This is because when we use reported speech, we are usually talking about a time in the past (because obviously the person who spoke originally spoke in the past). The verbs, therefore, usually have to be in the past too.

- Preeti said, "There is no one here."

becomes

- Preeti said that there was no one there.

When using reported speech, always watch out for place and time expressions.

- "I saw Himanshu in class yesterday," said Tom.
- Tom said that he saw Himanshu in class the previous day.

If you are not clear where the event took place, your sentence should read:

- Tom said that he saw Himanshu in class **that day.**

Similarly,

- Shruti said, "It is cold here."

becomes

- Shruti said that it was cold **there.**

# Direct and Indirect Speech

| Direct Speech | Reported Speech |
|---|---|
| today | that day |
| now | then |
| yesterday | the previous day |
| ... days ago | ... days earlier |
| last week | the week before |
| next year | the following year |
| tomorrow | the next day/the following day |
| here | there |
| this | that |
| these | those |

# Direct and Indirect Speech

When reporting speech, the tense usually changes. This is because when we use reported speech, we are usually talking about a time in the past (because obviously the person who spoke originally spoke in the past). The verbs, therefore, usually have to be in the past too.

## I Choose the correct reported speech version of each statement.

1 Tom said, "I want to visit my uncle this weekend."

*a* Tom said that he wants to visit his uncle that weekend. ☐

*b* Tom said that he wanted to visit his uncle that weekend. ☐

*c* Tom said that he wanted to visit his uncle this weekend. ☐

2 Horatio said, "I'm studying a lot at the moment."

*a* Horatio said that he was studying a lot at that moment. ☐

*b* Horatio said that he was studying a lot at the moment. ☐

*c* Horatio said that I was studying a lot at that moment. ☐

3 They said, "We've lived here for over ten years."

*a* They said that they have lived there for over ten years. ☐

*b* They said that they lived here for over ten years. ☐

*c* They said that they had lived there for over ten years. ☐

4 He asked me, "Have you finished reading the newspaper?"

*a* He asked me if had I finished reading the newspaper. ☐

*b* He asked me if I had finished reading the newspaper. ☐

*c* He asked me if I finished reading the newspaper. ☐

5 "I get up every morning at dawn," Pavel said.

*a* Pavel said that he got up every morning at dawn. ☐

*b* Pavel said I got up every morning at dawn. ☐

*c* Pavel said that he had got up every morning at dawn. ☐

# Direct and Indirect Speech

If we report something that is still true, it is not necessary to change the verb.

## I Choose the correct reported speech version of each statement.

1 She asked me, "When are we going home?"

- *a* She asked me when she was going home. ☐
- *b* She asked me when we were going home. ☐
- *c* She asked me when we are going to go home. ☐

2 She said, "I really wish I had bought that phone."

- *a* She told me that she really wished she bought that phone. ☐
- *b* She told me that she really had wished she had bought that phone. ☐
- *c* She told me that she really wished she had bought that phone. ☐

3 Creeley asked me, "Why do you want to be a poet?"

- *a* Creeley asked her why I wanted to be a poet. ☐
- *b* Creeley asked me why did I want to poet. ☐
- *c* Creeley asked me why I wanted to be a poet. ☐

4 Kairi asked her, "How long have you lived here?"

- *a* Kairi asked her how long she has lived there. ☐
- *b* Kairi asked her how long she lived there. ☐
- *c* Kairi asked her how long she had lived there. ☐

5 He said, "I must get going. Otherwise, I'm going to miss the train."

- *a* He told me that he had to get going. Otherwise, he was going to miss the train. ☐
- *b* He told me that he had to get going. Otherwise, I was going to miss the train. ☐
- *c* He told me that he must get going. Otherwise, he was going to miss the train. ☐

# Direct and Indirect Speech

Modal verbs **could**, **might**, **would**, **should**, **ought**, **had better** usually do not change in indirect speech.

## I Read the following commencement address, which was delivered by the comedian Jon Stewart at the William and Mary College, Virginia, United States in May 2004.

Thank you, Mr President, I had forgotten how crushingly dull these ceremonies are. Thank you.

My best to the choir. I have to say, that song never grows old for me. Whenever I hear that song, it reminds me of nothing.

I am honoured to be here. I do have a confession to make before we get going that I should explain very quickly. When I am not on television, this is actually how I dress. I apologize, but there's something very freeing about it. I congratulate the students for being able to walk even a half a mile in this non-breathable fabric in the Williamsburg heat. I am sure the environment that now exists under your robes, are the same conditions that primordial life began on this earth.

I know there were some parents that were concerned about my speech here tonight, and I want to assure you that you will not hear any language that is not common at, say, a dock workers' union meeting, or Tourette's convention, or profanity seminar. Rest assured.

I am honoured to be here and to receive this honorary doctorate. When I think back to the people that have been in this position before me from Benjamin Franklin to Queen Noor of Jordan, I can't help but wonder what has happened to this place. Seriously, it saddens me. As a person, I am honoured to get it; as an alumnus, I have to say I believe we can do better. And I believe we should. But it has always been a dream of mine to receive a doctorate and to know that today, without putting in any effort, I will. It's incredibly gratifying. Thank you. That's very nice of you, I appreciate it.

So if there's any real advice I can give you it's this. College is something you complete. Life is something you experience. So don't worry about your grade or the results or success. Success is defined in myriad ways, and you will find it, and people will no longer be grading you, but it will come from your own internal sense of decency which I imagine, after going through the programme here, is quite strong ...

Love what you do. Get good at it. Competence is a rare commodity in this day and age. And let the chips fall where they may ...

Thank you. Congratulations. I honour you. Good night.

# Direct and Indirect Speech

Always pay close attention to reflexive pronouns in direct speech. They should change to third person.

**II Imagine you were at the address. Write a letter to a friend who was not there about the speech. Use both direct and indirect speech in your letter.**

# Direct and Indirect Speech

When we are reporting things in the future or present perfect, we don't change the tense. For example: "I'll tell her you are coming."

**III What is the underlying message of this speech? Identify the key themes and ideas.**

**IV What is the tone of the speech? Is it positive or negative? Circle the adjectives and try to determine the tone.**

WORK SHEET 43

# Direct and Indirect Speech

When switching from indirect to direct speech, only provide the information we are given.

## I Fill in the blanks based on the given information.

1 "I have a meeting in the morning," he said.

He said that he ____________________ a meeting in the morning.

2 She realised: "I'm driving too fast!"

She realised that she ____________________ too fast.

3 I said, "Did you remember to call the bank?"

I asked ____________________ to call the bank.

4 "I haven't ordered my food yet."

I told you that I ____________________ my food yet.

5 She said: "I have been trying to get in touch with you all day."

She told me she ____________________ to get in touch with me all day.

6 He said, "I'll be organising it shortly."

He informed that he ____________________ it shortly.

7 He says: "I've friends and a job."

He says that he ____________________ and a job.

8 "Where do they live?" I asked.

I asked where they ____________________.

9 "Take a look at yourself in the mirror!" she said.

She ____________________ in the mirror.

10 Tom said, "I want to visit my friends this weekend."

Tom said he ____________________ his friends that weekend.

# Similes and Metaphors

A simile and metaphor are both comparisons between dissimilar objects that have one attribute or a group of attributes in common. In the case of a simile, this comparison is explicity spelt out, by using words such as **like** and **as**.

- She is **as** sweet as candy. He runs **like** a deer.
- She slept **like** a log. He is as thin **as** a stick.

In the case of a metaphor, the similarity is not spelt out. The dissimilar objects are juxtaposed or brought together in a manner that the reader is forced to perceive the common attributes.

- My dad is a bear.
- The bar of soap was a slippery eel.
- He hogged the road.
- She toyed with the idea.
- Her mind is like a sponge absorbing all the details.

We know that the girl's mind was not literally a sponge; however, because of memories and experiences, we are able to draw the conclusion that two things are being compared.

Writers use similes to explain things, to express emotion, and to make their writing more vivid and entertaining. Discovering fresh similes to use in your own writing also means discovering new ways of looking at your subjects.

# Similes and Metaphors

## Guide to Writing a Simile or a Metaphor

This guide might be as useful as a bucket in a rainstorm. Always remember, seemingly unconnected items can make great similes.

### Succinct

It should be short. If your simile is too long and complex, your reader might forget the point it was intended to make.

### Immediacy

It should bring an immediate image to the mind of the reader. Use everyday objects or known concepts. The more obscure the objects you are comparing, the more lost your reader will become.

### Commonality

It should refer to a common experience or image. A good simile should be understood by almost everyone, everywhere. The more specific the object, the fewer will be the people who recognise it.

### Relevance

Although a simile is not an exact description, it should be relevant. If we wanted to express that something was both large and immobile, a mountain would be a better object for comparison than a bus.

### Strength

A simile should strengthen the writing. If the simile adds nothing to the sense and clarity of the sentence, then we should not use it. If we simply wanted to say something was big without expressing the scale, then a simile becomes redundant.

A simile can affect how your reader views the subject. A badly crafted simile like the ones below can leave the reader feeling like she's just been kicked in the stomach by a yeti.

- Kiran fell seven storeys, hitting the pavement like a hefty bag filled with vegetable soup.
- John and Mary had never met. They were like two hummingbirds who had also never met.

LESSON 11

# Similes and Metaphors

He was as lame as a duck. Not the metaphorical lame duck either, but a real duck that was actually lame. Maybe from stepping on a land mine or something.

And because good, lyrical similes can inspire us, here are some famous similes from literature:

"Life is like an onion: You peel it off one layer at a time, and sometimes you weep."—Carl Sandburg

"She dealt with moral problems as a cleaver deals with meat."—James Joyce, "The Boarding House"

"Humanity, let us say, is like people packed in an automobile which is travelling downhill without lights at terrific speed and driven by a four-year-old child. The signposts along the way are all marked 'Progress.'"—Lord Dunsany

# Similes and Metaphors

A simile is a figure of speech involving the comparison of one thing with another thing of a different kind, used to make a description more emphatic or vivid.

**I Use the abstract and concrete nouns given below to create ten interesting similes of your own.**

| | |
|---|---|
| life | garbage can |
| love | chicken soup |
| happiness | revolving door |
| hope | eagle |
| friendship | banyan tree |
| hate | sand |
| family | puppy |
| beauty | mall |
| loneliness | rain |
| jealousy | sandwich |

Examples:

Life is like a garbage can, battered and full of rejection.

# Similes and Metaphors

Metaphors are figurative comparisons.

**I Find the simile or metaphor and underline it. Next, circle the objects being compared. Finally, write the meaning of the simile or metaphor based on the context of the sentence.**

1 The baby was like an octopus, grabbing at all the toys on the store shelves.

______________________________

2 As the teacher entered the room, she muttered under her breath, "This class is like a circus!"

______________________________

3 The giant's steps were thunder as he ran toward Jack.

______________________________

4 The pillow was a cloud when I put my head upon it after a rough day.

______________________________

5 I feel like a limp dishrag.

______________________________

6 Those girls are like two peas in a pod.

______________________________

7 The fluorescent light was like a thousand exploding suns during the exam.

______________________________

8 No one invites Harold to parties because he's a wet blanket.

______________________________

9 The bar of soap was a slippery eel during the dog's bath.

______________________________

10 I was as nervous as a cat with a long tail in a room full of rocking chairs.

______________________________

WORK SHEET 46

# Similes and Metaphors

Similes are literal comparisons using **like** or **as**.

## I Complete the similes to fill in the crossword.

**Across**

1 As ______________ as a feather.

3 Fly like a ______________ .

4 Swim like a ______________ .

7 Cry like a ______________ .

9 As ______________ as a bunny.

11 As ______________ as an ox.

12 As ______________ as an eel.

14 As slow as a ______________ .

7 As blind as a ______________ .

8 As ______________ as a mouse.

10 As ______________ as ice.

11 As ______________ as a fox.

13 Eat like a ______________ .

14 As white as ______________ .

**Down**

2 As tall as a ______________ .

3 As ______________ a bee.

5 As ______________ as a mule.

6 Waddle means to walk like a ______________ .

# Paragraph writing

We use a paragraph to explore or express an idea in detail. Like sentences, paragraphs also have a variety of styles. The style or 'type' of paragraph depends on the subject and the purpose.

## Narrative Paragraph

A narrative paragraph is the first part of telling a story or relating a sequence of events. It should introduce all the major elements of the plot such as character, setting, time and location. It should grip the reader from its introduction and proceed to 'narrate' or tell us the story.

A narrative essay can be descriptive, but the aim it to move the plot along. The narrative essay makes a point and that point is often defined in the opening sentence, but can also be found as the last sentence in the opening paragraph.

> My beautiful new watch had run eighteen months without losing or gaining, and without breaking any part of its machinery or stopping. I had come to believe it infallible in its judgments about the time of day, and to consider its constitution and its anatomy imperishable. But at last, one night, I let it run down. I grieved about it as if it were a recognised messenger and forerunner of calamity. But by and by I cheered up, set the watch by guess, and commanded my bodings and superstitions to depart. Next day I stepped into the chief jeweller's to set it by the exact time, and the head of the establishment took it out of my hand and proceeded to set it for me. Then he said, "She is four minutes slow – regulator wants pushing up." I tried to stop him – tried to make him understand that the watch kept perfect time. But no; all this human cabbage could see was that the watch was four minutes slow, and the regulator MUST be pushed up a little; and so, while I danced around him in anguish, and implored him to let the watch alone, he calmly and cruelly did the shameful deed. My watch began to gain. It gained faster and faster day by day. Within the week it sickened to a raging fever, and its pulse went up to a hundred and fifty in the shade.

Unlike descriptive writing, which simply attempts to describe a setting or scenario, narrative writing chronicles a sequence of events over a passage of time. In the above passage by Mark Twain, note how the passage of time is juxtaposed with the author's frame of mind. The tension in the story is being built while moving the plot along.

# Paragraph writing

## Guide to Writing a Narrative Paragraph

1. Remember to involve the readers in the story. It is much more interesting to actually recreate an incident for readers than to simply tell about it. This can be done by narrating the tale in the first person.
2. While the purpose of a narrative is to tell a story, details must be carefully selected to support, explain and enhance the story. Use vivid descriptions, metaphors and similes to help your reader visualise the scenario.
3. Leave out unnecessary details. Use visual language to describe the setting instead of boring your reader with a description of what was seen or heard.
4. Keep a close eye on the events taking place over time. Make a rough timeline of events to guide you while writing.
5. Narratives should include these story conventions: a plot, including setting and characters; an event or impending situation; and clear transitions of time.

# Paragraph writing

## I Write a narrative paragraph on any two of the topics given below. You may consider outside sources for help.

1 **Eureka Moment**—Think of an experience when you realised that you suddenly understood an idea, a skill, or a concept you had been struggling with—it can be related to class or a specific athletic skill you were trying to perfect. Write a narrative that tells the story of your moment of understanding. Your text should help readers understand how you felt to struggle with the idea or skill and then to master it.

2 **Nostalgia**—Choose a time from your childhood—You might think of the first time that you rode the school bus, the first test you ever took and so on. Narrate the events related to the childhood memory that you've chosen so that your readers will understand why the event was important and memorable.

3 **The Good, the Bad and Story**—Think about an event in your life that seemed terrible but turned out to be good. Tell the story of the event that you experienced and help your readers understand how an event that seemed negative turned out to have valuable consequences.

4 **Standing Up**—Think of a time when you did something that took a lot of nerve, a time when you didn't follow the crowd or a time when you stood up for your beliefs. Whatever you choose, think about the details of the event and write a story that tells about what happened. Your narrative should show your readers why you decided to make a stand or try something that took nerve, give specifics on the events and share how you felt after the event.

# Paragraph writing

# Essay

Often you will have to write on a subject that cannot be summed up an in a single paragraph. The trick to writing a multi-paragraph essay is to structure your argument or story before you begin.

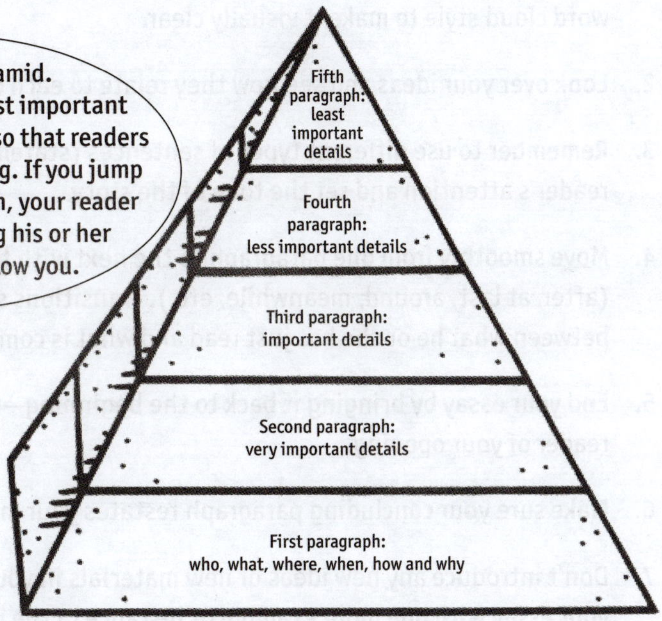


## Brainstorming

Before writing, make a list of all the things you want to include in your paragraph.

Do you need to do more research? Are all your points correct?

As you write, pay attention to the content. Do you answer the five Ws of descriptive writing?

The five Ws are:

Who

What

Why

Where

When

LESSON 13

# Essay

## Tips for Essay Writing

1. Organise the information you have before writing. Make notes or write complete sentences. Use a word cloud style to make it visually clear.
2. Look over your ideas and see how they relate to each other. Group them in a logical order.
3. Remember to use different types of sentences (statement, command, exclamation) to engage the reader's attention and set the tone of the story.
4. Move smoothly from one paragraph to the next with the help of transitional words and phrases (after, at last, around, meanwhile, etc.). Transitions show the reader that there is a connection between what he or she has just read and what is coming in the next paragraph.
5. End your essay by bringing it back to the beginning—write a closing paragraph that reminds your reader of your opening.
6. Make sure your concluding paragraph restates your main idea so your reader isn't left hanging.
7. Don't introduce any new ideas or new materials in your final paragraph. However, you can close your essay with one more example or instance of the main idea.
8. After you have written your last sentence to your closing paragraph, you have only one more thing to write: the title.
9. Although the title is the first thing people read, many writers wait until the end to name their essay. Your title should give you reader some idea of your subject, details and the tone of your subject.
10. Don't give away too much in the title. Where long titles are acceptable for researched, scientific essays, other kinds of essays and stories should have short descriptive titles.

WORK SHEET 48

# Essay

But wait, before you turn in your masterpiece to your teacher or friend, read the list below and see if your essay meets all the criteria listed.

## Evaluation Checklist

Yes ☐ No ☐ Does my title grab the reader's attention?

Yes ☐ No ☐ Does my introduction draw the reader into the essay?

Yes ☐ No ☐ Does the opening paragraph give a clear idea about the subject?

Yes ☐ No ☐ Is every group of words a complete and concise sentence?

Yes ☐ No ☐ Are my ideas organised in a way that will make sense to my reader?

Yes ☐ No ☐ Is each paragraph clearly linked to the paragraph before and after it?

Yes ☐ No ☐ Does my conclusion restate my main idea?

Yes ☐ No ☐ Does my concluding paragraph give my reader a sense of closure?

# Essay

**I Write an essay on any one of the topics given below. Your essay should run no longer than three or four paragraphs.**

**1 Your Favourite Television Show**

Most, if not all of us, have grown up watching television and have our own favourite shows. Pick a television show that you enjoy (or enjoyed, it doesn't have to be current) and introduce the show to a friend who has never seen or heard of it. Explain why you enjoy the show and what are some of its highlights and weaknesses (try to use specific examples). Here are a few questions to help you get started:

a. What type of show is it (sitcom, drama, reality, etc.)?

b. What is the premise of the show (plot, characters, location)?

c. What specifically about this show appeals to you?

d. What are the criticisms that you can offer about it (weak acting, convoluted plot, etc.)?

e. Why should someone watch it?

Do not write a review of the show, but do give a quick description of its basic plot and style. You may consider opening your essay with why this show is your favourite or how you first began watching it.

**2 A Hero for Our Time**

Who is it that inspires you? Write an essay on a person or historical figure that has had an impact on your life. A few ideas to explore could be:

a. Is this person fictional or real?

b. What about this person do you admire?

c. What are some of the ways in which your life can be said to reflect his/her teachings or principles.

d. What sets this person apart from the rest?

WORK SHEET 49

# Essay

LESSON 14

# Book Review

A book review (or book report) is a form of writing in which a book is analysed based on content and style. It can be as short as a sentence ("This book was so boring that I had to pull out a tooth to stay awake") to a substantial essay. Such a review often contains evaluations of the book on the basis of personal taste. In short, a book review is simply your thoughts on a book you've read that encourages or discourages another person from reading the same book.

There may be different ways of reviewing a book.

> *Harry Potter and the Philosopher's Stone* is the first novel in the Harry Potter series written by J. K. Rowling and featuring Harry Potter, a young wizard. It describes how Harry discovers he is a wizard, makes close friends and a few enemies at the Hogwarts School of Witchcraft and Wizardry, and with the help of his friends thwarts an attempted comeback by the evil wizard Voldemort, who killed Harry's parents and tried to kill Harry when he was a year old.
>
> The series is extremely popular and has several awards and included on the *New York Times* bestseller lists.
>
> Most critics complimented Rowling's imagination, humour, simple, direct style and clever plot construction, although a few complained that the final books felt rushed. The writing has been compared to that of Jane Austen, one of Rowling's favourite authors, and of Roald Dahl, whose works dominated children's stories before the appearance of Harry Potter. While a few critics thought the book looked backwards to the boarding school stories of Enid Blyton, others thought it placed the genre firmly in the modern world by featuring contemporary ethical and social issues.

The above review is called a formal review. It summarises the plot of *Harry Potter and the Philosopher's Stone*, introduces the major characters and extols the popularity of the book. The style is mostly factual and indicates that the reviewer did additional research or reading before writing the review.

# Book Review

A less formal review of the same book might run like this:

Harry Potter has lived a dismal life with his aunt and uncle, the Dursleys. He sleeps in a closet and has never had a birthday party or Christmas presents. Even worse, he has to endure life with his horrible spoiled cousin, Dudley. Then on Harry's eleventh birthday, things change when a letter arrives (by owl), inviting him to attend the Hogwarts School of Witchcraft and Wizardry. Suddenly Harry finds himself among friends, learning about potion-making and magic-wand waving and broomstick riding.

There are chocolate frogs and Every Flavour Beans and a three-headed dog and Quidditch—a game better than soccer. Also, Hagrid, a lovable gamekeeper who befriends Harry; Hermione Granger, a witch who's read all the school books and knows all the rules; and there's Ron Weasley, Harry's best friend who has quite a legacy of his own to fill. Hogwarts treats him well, even with the abominable Malfoy's mean tricks or Professor Snape's obvious hatred of Harry. Soon Harry finds himself in the middle of a mystery at Hogwarts, and together with his two new friends, embarks on adventures he never dreamed possible.

*Harry Potter and the Philosopher's Stone* is engaging with its imagery, humour, plot twists and real-life child problems. The book not only appeals to children but to adults as well. J. K. Rowling is a master of fantasy. She really can, with no difficulty at all, think herself back to eleven years old. You will love the whimsical descriptions, humorous quotes and the fun characters.

**Circle the adjectives. How many are they? Are most of them positive or negative? What overall emotion do you get from reading this review? If you have read the book, do you agree with the reviewer?**

The above review doesn't tell us any additional details about the book (when it was published, how many books are in the series, if it is even part of a series, etc.) but contains the reviewer's reaction to the book. This kind of review makes clear what the reviewers feels about a book, but often neglects to point out any negative (if any) points of the work.

# Book Review

The following review of *Harry Potter and the Deathly Hallows* is clearly written by a fan of the Harry Potter series. But she/he doesn't seem to be very happy with it. Why might that be?

I know many people will disagree with this review, so I prepare myself at the outset for a barrage of complaints and angry e-mails.

*Harry Potter and the Deathly Hallows* provides pretty much everything we've been promised from the outset: an ending, and a satisfying one at that—but not without its price. Many beloved characters die, and some of them die "off page" as it were, so that we readers aren't even privy to the details of their deaths, or their final moments of life. Some of these deaths will bring tears to the eyes of any Harry Potter devotee, I've no doubt of that. But as for the main death, the one so many have wondered about? Well, that's where Rowling falls back on a few too-worn literary devices, and where she loses us.

I found this book to be far too full of easy short cuts and simplistic clichés to give it five stars. Far too often, Harry and his friends were "mysteriously" saved at the last minute. This is too frustrating. Perhaps it's unfair to criticize Rowling for the intelligence of her fans, but the fact is that many of her secrets have been guessed. In fact, the few that haven't seem only to surprise because Rowling conveniently has them pop up for the first time in this book. Magical objects we've seen many times before suddenly have new and useful—and VERY convenient—magical properties. People we've only heard of have convenient new information and relevance to the plot.

A book this long that purports to be the end of an epic series should not have this many plot holes and inexplicable events. I was also sorely disappointed to realise that she left out a number of things she promised fans would be included in this book. For instance, many fans have asked her what Harry's parents did for a living. She always said she couldn't tell us because it would be too big a plot spoiler for the upcoming novels. Well, now the novels are all finished and we still don't know. Why didn't she include that in this final book, if it really was supposed to matter so much?

There is no doubt that in Harry Potter Rowling has created a brave and endurable hero, one who will linger in the hearts and minds of readers for generations to come. But in this humble reader's opinion, she has also created one for whom the struggle ended a bit too quickly and easily, of whom too many things are left unknown, and for whom answers and help came too readily and too conveniently in the end.

# Book Review

**I** Do you agree with the third review? Why? What might you have written differently?

**II** Who is the "us" the author often refers to? On whose behalf is this review written?

**III** Make two separate lists of all the positive things the author mentions about the book. Now make a list of all the negative things.

# Book Review

**IV** Do you feel the reviewer's complaint is justified? Why?

**V** Of the three reviews you have read, which did you like and why?

# Book Review

**I** **Write a review of a book written by your favourite author.**

# Revision 2

## I Read the following extract by Paro Anand and follow the exercises given.

New uniform—turquoise blue pinafore with white shirt. New bags—with diagonal streaks of purple and pink. New books—strange new books with histories and geographies I knew nothing about. New school—named The Convent of Bukit Nanas, which meant literally the convent on the hill of pineapples—weird! Yes, that's how it felt now. New country, new language, new school, new faces, new everything. Except, maybe, come to think of it, perhaps everything was old and it was just me who was new. New and unfamiliar.

The big, black gates shut with a clang. Shutting my mother and me in. My heart was sinking and skipping at the same time, which is something that always gives me hiccups. A most inauspicious start. I turned back to see my mother mouthing, "best of luck, *bacche*," (of course, I was still *bacche* or even *chottu* to my mom, although I was fifteen, but I guess all moms are the same, you're always a baby to them). Then I was led away, through the school portals by a sweet, round-faced Malaysian Chinese nun.

**1** Identify the various elements of descriptive writing. What adjective and adverbs are being used with which nouns. What is the overall effect?

______________________________________________

______________________________________________

______________________________________________

______________________________________________

______________________________________________

______________________________________________

**2** Write short sentences for each of the nouns being described, for example, the uniform was new. It was turquoise blue with a white shirt, etc.

______________________________________________

______________________________________________

______________________________________________

# Revision 2

**3 Imagine the sentences without adjectives or adjectival clauses. What difference do you notice to the story?**

**4 Write a third paragraph continuing from where the last one left off.**

# Revision 2

## II Read the following excerpt from Siddhartha Sarma's action-packed *The Grasshopper's Run*.

It was now the morning after he had arrived. He had not gone running at dawn. He was at the range, with the Lee-Enfield, half a box of cartridges, a glass bottle of Spencer's Gun Cleaner—a fluid which was difficult to get and which KC had told him to use sparingly—a ramrod and a flannel rag, rolls of hospital cotton, a wooden ruler, a protractor and his notebook.

The sun was coming up in a mild way, and it was cool in the hollow. He was lying on his bare stomach on one of the boards at the firing platform, which was angled a little upwards and level with the targets. The gun rested on a sack of thickly packed sand, which kept it steady but prevented the barrel from shuddering with the recoil.

His legs were stretched straight and a little wide behind him, and he was wearing shoes so his toes would not bend, because he had discovered that if they stayed bent inward for too long—which happened in this position—they started quivering.

The long stock of the rifle was pressed against the platelike muscles which were beginning to form between his upper right chest and shoulders. His left hand was stretched straight against the platform and held up the barrel in the centre of his palm. The elbow was hard against the platform. He was looking along the rear sight, a pointed knob in this older version of the rifle, down to the front sight, a trident; the rear knob and central spike of the trident on the edge of the barrel lining up against the centre of the cross on the target, which at this distance was just barely distinct, but distinct nonetheless. His short neck was still, his left eye closed, his right eye on the front sight.

At this distance, he had discovered that he need not hold half his breath in, because for an accurate shooter, that much stillness of the upper body, for that distance, came naturally. Competition shooters, he had been told, considered this distance barely worth the bother. He remembered something the planter had told him at his house, a quote by a famous American competition shooter. That gent had remarked once, according to the papers: "Two hundred yards? Why, at that range, I don't need a rifle. I might as well punch the target down."

1 What is the mood of the passage? What are some of the emotions you felt as you read this?

___

___

___

# Revision 2

**2** **What do you think is happening? What happens next?**

**3** **"Two hundred yards? Why, at that range, I don't need a rifle. I might as well punch the target down." What do you think the American shooter meant by this statement?**

**4** **Imagine that this passage is about you. Now write a letter to your friend describing your morning.**

# Revision 2

## III Read the following exerpt from the story "Haro Babu the Gentleman" by Shirshendu Mukhopadhyay.

Haro Babu sensed that a burglar had entered his house. So he sat up on his bed and murmured, "This is outrageous behaviour!"

Very irritated, he got up from his bed. He opened the door of his room, went out onto the balcony, and gazed at the moonlight quietly. He disliked burglary very much. It was not possible for him to stand the sight of a burglar robbing his house under his own nose.

The burglar was quite shameless. He was not even trying to hide the sinful act that he was engaged in. From the balcony, Haro Babu could hear horrible noises of boxes being moved, utensils falling, cupboards being broken in.

Angrily he turned his face towards the room and shouted, "Not so loud! Shameless idiot!"

The thief, or maybe the thieves, took the hint and refrained from making loud noises. But it was taking them ages to finish their act. The burglars these days were mere novices. They would not learn their trade properly, and get to work only after a few days of training.

1 What is the mood of this passage? Can you gauge the tone?

______________________________________________

______________________________________________

______________________________________________

______________________________________________

______________________________________________

______________________________________________

______________________________________________

2 What are some of the words that indicate the mood and tone?

______________________________________________

______________________________________________

3 "The burglars these days were mere novices." What does this statement mean? What does this say about Haro Babu?

4 What do you think happens next?

# Revision 2

**5 Imagine you are the burglar. Write an essay about your strange experience robbing Haro Babu.**

# WORD BANKS Verb Tense

Tenses allow speakers and writers to express exactly what they want to say.

## Present Tense Verbs

| Tense | Number | 1st Person | 2nd Person | 3rd Person |
|---|---|---|---|---|
| *Simple present* | Singular | I **eat** fish. | You **eat** fish. | He/she/it **eats** fish. |
| | Plural | We **eat** fish. | You **eat** fish. | They **eat** fish. |
| *Present continuous* | Singular | I **am eating** fish. | You **are eating** fish. | He/she/it **is eating** fish. |
| | Plural | We **are eating** fish. | You **are eating** fish. | They **are eating** fish. |
| *Present perfect* | Singular | I **have eaten** fish. | You **have eaten** fish. | He/she/it **has eaten** fish. |
| | Plural | We **have eaten** fish. | You **have eaten** fish. | They **have eaten** fish. |
| *Perfect continuous* | Singular | I **have been eating** fish. | You **have been eating** fish. | He/she/it **has been eating** fish. |
| | Plural | We **have been eating** fish. | You **have been eating** fish. | They **have been eating** fish. |

## Past Tense Verbs

| Tense | Number | 1st Person | 2nd Person | 3rd Person |
|---|---|---|---|---|
| *Simple past* | Singular | I **ate** fish. | You **ate** fish. | He/she/it **ate** fish. |
| | Plural | We **ate** fish. | You **ate** fish. | They **ate** fish. |
| *Past continuous* | Singular | I **was eating** fish. | You **were eating** fish. | He/she/it **was eating** fish. |
| | Plural | We **were eating** fish. | You **were eating** fish. | They **were eating** fish. |
| *Past perfect* | Singular | I **had eaten** fish. | You **had eaten** fish. | He/she/it **had eaten** fish. |
| | Plural | We **had eaten** fish. | You **had eaten** fish. | They **had eaten** fish. |
| *Perfect continuous* | Singular | I **had been eating** fish. | You **had been eating** fish. | He/she/it **had been eating** fish. |
| | Plural | We **had been eating** fish. | You **had been eating** fish. | They **had been eating** fish. |

## Future Tense Verbs

| Tense | Number | 1st Person | 2nd Person | 3rd Person |
|---|---|---|---|---|
| *Simple future* | Singular | I **will eat** fish. | You **will eat** fish. | He/she/it **will eat** fish. |
| | Plural | We **will eat** fish. | You **will eat** fish. | They **will eat** fish. |

| | | | | |
|---|---|---|---|---|
| *Future continuous* | Singular | I **will be eating** fish. | You **will be eating** fish. | He/she/it **will be eating** fish. |
| | Plural | We **will be eating** fish. | You **will be eating** fish. | They **will be eating** fish. |
| *Future perfect* | Singular | I **will have eaten** fish. | You **will have eaten** fish. | He/she/it **will have eaten** fish. |
| | Plural | We **will have eaten** fish. | You **will have eaten** fish. | They **will have eaten** fish. |
| *Future Perfect continuous* | Singular | I **will have been eating** fish. | You **will have been eating** fish. | He/she/it **will have been eating** fish. |
| | Plural | We **will have been eating** fish. | You **will have been eating** fish. | They **will have been eating** fish. |

We can even add other verbs to clarify our meaning.

→ I ***could*** have been eating fish.

→ He ***might*** have eaten fish.

→ They ***should*** be eating fish.

→ We ***can*** eat fish.

## Verbs

Auxiliary verbs are helping verbs. They provide extra information about a sentence, which is not given by the main verb.

List of helping (**auxiliary**) verbs

- am, aren't (only in inversion, as in aren't I special?), 'm (as in I'm)
- be
- can, can't
- did, didn't
- does, doesn't
- has, hasn't, 's (→ She's gone out.)
- is, isn't, 's (→ She's back.)
- might, mightn't
- ought, oughtn't
- should, shouldn't
- were, weren't
- would, wouldn't, 'd (→ I'd go out.)
- are, aren't, 're (as in you're)
- been
- could, couldn't
- do, don't
- had, hadn't, 'd (→ She'd gone out.)
- have, haven't, 've (→ I've)
- may, mayn't
- must, mustn't
- shall, shan't
- was, wasn't
- will, won't, 'll (→ she'll)

# WORD BANKS Verb Tense

## Irregular Verbs

One of the more frustrating things about tenses is learning the irregular verbs by heart. As you know, the past tense forms of regular verbs end in **ed** or **d**, however, irregular verbs just need to be learnt.

| Infinitive | Past simple | Past participle |
|---|---|---|
| be | was/were | been |
| beat | beat | beaten |
| become | became | become |
| begin | began | begun |
| bend | bent | bent |
| bet | bet | bet |
| bite | bit | bitten |
| blow | blew | blown |
| break | broke | broken |
| bring | brought | brought |
| build | built | built |
| burst | burst | burst |
| buy | bought | bought |
| catch | caught | caught |
| choose | chose | chosen |
| come | came | come |
| cost | cost | cost |
| cut | cut | cut |
| deal | dealt | dealt |
| dig | dug | dug |
| do | did | done |
| draw | drew | drawn |
| drink | drank | drunk |
| drive | drove | driven |
| eat | ate | eaten |
| fall | fell | fallen |

| Infinitive | Past simple | Past participle |
|---|---|---|
| feed | fed | fed |
| feel | felt | felt |
| fight | fought | fought |
| find | found | found |
| fly | flew | flown |
| forbid | forbade | forbidden |
| forget | forgot | forgotten |
| freeze | froze | frozen |
| get | got | got |
| give | gave | given |
| go | went | gone |
| grow | grew | grown |
| hang | hung | hung |
| have | had | had |
| hear | heard | heard |
| hide | hid | hidden |
| hit | hit | hit |
| hold | held | held |
| hurt | hurt | hurt |
| keep | kept | kept |
| know | knew | known |
| lay | laid | laid |
| lead | led | led |
| leave | left | left |
| lend | lent | lent |
| let | let | let |

# WORD BANKS Verb Tense

| Infinitive | Past simple | Past participle |
|---|---|---|
| lie | lay | lain |
| light | lit | lit |
| lose | lost | lost |
| make | made | made |
| mean | meant | meant |
| meet | met | met |
| pay | paid | paid |
| put | put | put |
| read | read | read |
| ride | rode | ridden |
| ring | rang | rung |
| rise | rose | risen |
| run | ran | run |
| say | said | said |
| see | saw | seen |
| seek | sought | sought |
| sell | sold | sold |
| send | sent | sent |
| set | set | set |
| sew | sewed | sewn/sewed |
| shake | shook | shaken |
| shine | shone | shone |
| shoot | shot | shot |
| show | showed | shown |
| shrink | shrank | shrunk |
| shut | shut | shut |
| sing | sang | sung |
| sink | sank | sunk |

| Infinitive | Past simple | Past participle |
|---|---|---|
| sit | sat | sat |
| sleep | slept | slept |
| speak | spoke | spoken |
| spend | spent | spent |
| split | split | split |
| spread | spread | spread |
| spring | sprang | sprung |
| stand | stood | stood |
| steal | stole | stolen |
| stick | stuck | stuck |
| sting | stung | stung |
| stink | stank | stunk |
| strike | struck | struck |
| swear | swore | sworn |
| sweep | swept | swept |
| swim | swam | swum |
| swing | swung | swung |
| take | took | taken |
| teach | taught | taught |
| tear | tore | torn |
| tell | told | told |
| think | thought | thought |
| throw | threw | thrown |
| understand | understood | understood |
| wake | woke | woken |
| wear | wore | worn |
| win | won | won |
| write | wrote | written |

# WORD BANKS Pronoun

A pronoun is a substitute for a noun. Some pronouns are: **I**, **me**, **she**, **he**, **her**, **him**, **it**, **you**, **they** and **them.**

| Pronouns | Pronoun as subject | Pronoun as object | Pronoun as possessive adjective | Possessive pronoun | Reflexive pronoun |
|---|---|---|---|---|---|
| 1st Person Singular | I | me | my | mine | myself |
| 2nd Person Singular | you | you | your | yours | yourself |
| 3rd Person Singular | he<br>she<br>it | him<br>her<br>it | his<br>her<br>it | his<br>hers<br>its | himself<br>herself<br>itself |
| 1st Person Plural | we | us | our | ours | ourselves |
| 2nd Person Plural | you | you | your | yours | yourselves |
| 3rd Person Plural | they | them | their | theirs | themselves |

## Irregular Plural Nouns

| Singural | Plural | Singural | Plural | Singural | Plural |
|---|---|---|---|---|---|
| alumnus | alumni | thesis | theses | phenomenon | phenomena |
| cactus | cacti | appendix | appendices | stratum | strata |
| focus | foci/focuses | index | indeces/indexes | deer | deer |
| fungus | fungi/funguses | matrix | matrices/matrixes | fish | fish |
| nucleus | nuclei | beau | beaux | means | means |
| radius | radii | bureau | bureaus/bureaux | offspring | offspring |
| stimulus | stimuli | tableau | tableaux/tableaus | series | series |
| axis | axes | child | children | sheep | sheep |
| analysis | analyses | man | men | species | species |
| basis | bases | ox | oxen | foot | feet |
| crisis | crises | woman | women | goose | geese |
| diagnosis | diagnoses | bacterium | bacteria | tooth | teeth |
| ellipsis | ellipses | corpus | corpora | antenna | antennae/antennas |
| hypothesis | hypotheses | criterion | criteria | formula | formulae/formulas |
| oasis | oases | curriculum | curricula | nebula | nebulae |
| paralysis | paralyses | datum | data | vertebra | vertebrae |
| parenthesis | parentheses | genus | genera | vita | vitae |
| synthesis | syntheses | medium | media | louse | lice |
| synopsis | synopses | memorandum | memoranda | mouse | mice |

## Pronouns Vocabulary Word List

| | | | |
|---|---|---|---|
| **A** | **I** | **O** | **U** |
| all | I | one | us |
| another | it | other | **W** |
| any | its | others | we |
| anybody | itself | our | what |
| anyone | **M** | ours | whatever |
| anything | many | ourselves | which |
| **B** | me | **S** | whichever |
| both | mine | several | who |
| **E** | more | she | whoever |
| each | most | some | whom |
| either | much | somebody | whomever |
| everybody | my | someone | whose |
| everyone | myself | something | **Y** |
| everything | **N** | **T** | you |
| **F** | neither | that | your |
| few | no one | their | yours |
| **H** | nobody | theirs | yourself |
| he | none | them | |
| her | nothing | themselves | |
| hers | | these | |
| herself | | they | |
| him | | this | |
| himself | | those | |
| his | | | |

# WORD BANKS Punctuation

### ' Apostrophe

An apostrophe can show ownership or missing letters (it is – it's). For ownership, the rules are:

Singular owners add: 's.

Plural owners not ending in 's' add: 's.

Plural owners ending in 's', add: s'.

➩ The monkey snapped my car's antenna and stabbed me with it.

### ( ) Brackets

Brackets contain a piece of additional information put into the main sentence. We can also use commas to do this job.

➩ The baby (when he is hungry) will bite my finger.

### : Colon

A colon introduces more information. This information may be a list or a second clause adding information to the first clause.

➩ These animals are not edible: camels, kangaroos and parrots.

### , Comma

A comma separates parts of a sentence and can be similar to a pause in speech.

➩ Although nobody is looking at him, the panda is still hiding in the corner.

### — Dash

A dash is used in informal writing.

➩ That hat looks great – everyone will love it.

### ... Ellipsis

Ellipsis is the name for three dots that show the writing is incomplete.

➩ The lion leapt towards the unsuspecting visitor and before you knew it ...

## 10. Apostrophes

Apostrophes have two functions: to show contractions (**I won't**) and possession (**Shakespeare's tragedy**). They are not used to show the plural of a noun.

| | |
|---|---|
| My novel's cover contains numerous inaccuracies. ✔ | My novels cover contains numerous inaccuracies. ✘ |
| For now, the terrorists threats have not cowed the community. ✘ | For now, the terrorists' threats have not cowed the community. ✔ |

## 9. Nouns ending in y

Nouns ending in **y** often produce similar confusion with regard to possession. If you want to talk about something belonging to a country, for instance, write **country's**, not **countries.**

## 8. Conjunction confusion

Conjunctions like *and*, *but* and *for* join independent clauses. Students often use *however*, *therefore*, and *thus* as if they were conjunctions, but they are not. They're adverbs, and can't connect independent clauses—you'll still need a semicolon or period.

| | |
|---|---|
| I studied for hours but he never opened a book—and we both topped the exam. ✘ | I studied for hours but he never opened a book yet we both topped the exam. ✔ |

It's usually more graceful to place *however*, *therefore*, and similar words not right at the beginning but at some convenient pause later on:

| |
|---|
| Truth is a good thing; it is not, however, the highest political good. |

## 7. Infamy and notoriety

*Infamous* is not a fancy way of saying famous. It means the opposite: famously wicked or bad. Gandhi was famous; Hitler was infamous. Likewise, *notoriety* doesn't mean just being widely known—it means being known for being bad

| | |
|---|---|
| Although cryogenics was introduced over a decade ago, it is only now receiving the notoriety it deserves. ✘ | Although cryogenics was introduced over a decade ago, it is only now receiving the attention it deserves. ✔ |

## 6. Practice and practise

In many English-speaking countries (UK, Australia, India and Canada) **practice** is the noun, **practise** the verb. However, in the US, the spelling **practice** is more often used for both the noun and the verb.

| | |
|---|---|
| You need to practise your English. ✔ | You need to practice your English. ✔ |

### 5. Advice and advise

Advice is a noun and advise is the verb form and you clearly have to use the noun before the adjective.

| | |
|---|---|
| She gave me very good advise on buying a car. ✗ | She gave me very good advice on buying a car. ✔ |

### 4. Intents and purposes

Not intensive purposes.

| | |
|---|---|
| For all intensive purposes, Apple has won the computer wars. ✗ | For all intents and purposes, Apple has won the phone wars. ✔ |

### 3. Of or Off

People often use these words interchangeably, but each has its own correct usage. It helps to think of it like this: ***Of*** implies belonging to something or coming from. ***Off*** implies to be removed, away from or less. **Dispose of** is an exception.

| | |
|---|---|
| The car went of the road. ✗ | The car went off the road. ✔ |

### 2. Principal/principle

Principal is an adjective meaning **foremost** or **most important**, while principle is a noun meaning **guiding idea.**

| | |
|---|---|
| The Constitution of India lays down the fundamental rights and principals of citizens. ✗ | The Constitution of India lays down the fundamental rights and principles of citizens. ✔ |

### 1. It's/its

Because apostrophes are used for possession as well as contraction, many students get confused about the distinction between them. Remember that **it's** is a contraction, not a possessive: *It's = it is*. *It*, like other pronouns (*he, his; she, her*) doesn't take an apostrophe to show possession:

| | |
|---|---|
| The baby howled when I stole it's toy. ✗ | The baby howled when I stole its toy. ✔ |

*Who's* and *whose* have the same distinction. *Who's* is a contraction of **who is** or, less commonly, **who has. Whose** is the possessive of **who.**

| | |
|---|---|
| Whose ready to go out tonight? ✗ | Who's ready to go out tonight? ✔ |

# WORD BANKS Homographs

words that are identical with another in spelling but different in meaning.

angle
arms
back
ball
bank
bar
bark
base
bat
bay
beam
bear
beat
bill
bit
blind
block
blow
board
booty
bow
brand
cape
case
cast
change
charge
chop
club
coach
coat
coast
cold
column
corn

count
court
craft
crane
cricket
crop
cross
crow
dock
down
draught
draw
drill
drive
drone
duck
express
fair
fast
felt
file
fill
fine
fire
fit
flag
fleet
float
fold
foot
form
game
gape
grain
grate

grave
ground
gum
hail
hamper
hand
hide
hit
hold
host
iron
jam
jar
joint
jumper
June
just
kid
kind
kite
lap
last
lay
lead
lean
leaves
left
let
letter
lie
lift
light
line
list
litter

lock
log
mail
march
mass
master
match
may
mean
might
mine
mint
mould
mount
nail
nature
note
order
organ
page
palm
pass
patient
peal
plot
plug
pole
port
post
pound
power
private
prune
pupil
race

range
rank
record
rent
rest
rifle
right
ring
rock
roll
rose
round
row
ruler
rung
sack
safe
save
scale
scales
seal
season
shed
sheet
sign
sink
smoke
soil
sound
sow
speaker
spell
spoke
spring
squash

staff
stage
stall
stand
star
state
steer
stern
stick
stock
stole
strike
stud
stump
suit
swallow
swift
table
tear
temper
tile
till
top
train
trip
tumbler
turn
vote
wake
watch
wave
well
wind
work
yawn

# WORD BANKS Homophones

ail / ale
air / heir
aisle / isle / I'll
allowed / aloud
alter / altar
arc / ark
arms / alms
ascent / assent
ate / eight
aunt / aren't
awe / or / oar / ore
bail / bale
bald / bawled
bare / bear
bark / barque
barren / baron
base / bass
be / bee
beach / beech
been / bean
beer / bier
bell / belle
berry / bury
birth / berth
bite / bight
blew / blue
boar / bore
board / bored
boarder / border
bold / bowled
born / borne
bough / bow
bow / beau
boy / buoy
braid / brayed
braise / brays
brake / break
bread / bred
brews / bruise
bridal / bridle
but / butt
buy / by / bye
cannon / canon

canvas / canvass
capital / capitol
carrot / carat
cast / caste
caw / core / corps
cede / seed
ceiling / sealing
cellar / seller
cent / scent / sent
centred / scented
cents / scents / sense
cereal / serial
cheap / cheep
check / cheque
chews / choose
choral / coral
cite / sight / site
clause / claws
coarse / course
coat / cote
colonel / kernel
council / counsel
creak / creek
crews / cruise
cue / queue
curb / kerb
currant / current
cygnet / signet
days / daze
dear / deer
dew / due
die / dye
died / dyed
dies / dyes
doe / dough
draft / draught
draw / drawer
dying / dyeing
earn / urn
ewe / you / yew
ewes / use
eye / I
eyelet / islet

faint / feint
fair / fare
farther / father
fate / fete
feat / feet
find / fined
fir / fur
flaw / floor
flea / flee
flew / flu / flue
flocks / phlox
flow / floe
flower / flour
for / fore / four
fort / fought
foul / fowl
frays / phrase
freeze / frieze
gait / gate
gamble / gambol
genes / jeans
gild / guild
gnaw / nor
gored / gourd
gorilla / guerrilla
grate / great
grater / greater
groan / grown
guest / guessed
hail / hale
hanger / hangar
hart / heart
heal / heel / he'll
hear / here
heard / herd
hears / here's
hew / hue
higher / hire
him / hymn
ho / hoe
hoard / horde
hoarse / horse
hose / hoes

hole / whole
holy / wholly
hour / our
idle / idol
in / inn
island / Ireland
jam / jamb
key / quay
knave / nave
knead / need / kneed
knew / new
knight / night
knot / not
know / no
knows / nose
lacks / lax
lain / lane
laps / lapse
larva / lava
lead / led
leak / leek
lessen / lesson
liar / lyre
licence / license
lieu / loo / Lou
lightening / lightning
links / lynx
load / lode
loan / lone
loot / lute
made / maid
mail / male
main / mane
maize / maze
mall / maul
manner / manor
mantel / mantle
mare / mayor
marshal / martial
meat / meet / mete
medal / meddle
metal / mettle
metre / meter

# Evaluation Sheet

Name: ______________________

Date: ______________________

| Criterion | Superior | Satisfactory | Meets requirements | Unsatisfactory |
|---|---|---|---|---|
| Each assignment conveys a clear and specific purpose | | | | |
| The student selects facts and composes genres that fit with his or her overall purpose and framing context | | | | |
| The student successfully identifies and employs the conventions of each chosen genre | | | | |
| The student places and organises his or her arguments logically | | | | |
| The student shows connections between different points to support and develop his or her ideas | | | | |
| The student demonstrates his or her ability to research, select and integrate sources | | | | |
| The student offers sufficient evidence and explanation to develop his or her main ideas in each genre | | | | |

This sheet evaluates the student's writing skills.

Notes: